MY CONFESSIONAL

MY CONFESSIONAL

JANET DEVLIN

OMNIBUS PRESS

London / New York / Paris / Sydney / Copenhagen / Berlin / Madrid / Tokyo

This book is dedicated to the Do Crew, for keeping my dream alive
— I couldn't do do do do it without you.

Copyright © 2020 Omnibus Press
(A Division of Music Sales Limited)

Cover designed by Amazing15
Picture research by the author

ISBN: 978-1-913172-24-4

Disclaimer: Names, dates and minor details included in some chapters have been altered in order to protect the identities of those involved.

Designed and Typeset by Evolution Design and Digital Limited (Kent)
Printed in the Czech Republic

A catalogue record for this book is available from the British Library.

CONTENTS

PREFACE

Before you descend down the rabbit hole that is my life, I must first make one thing clear: this book comes with one giant trigger warning. Although I've tried to ensure this book never became a guide book for self-destruction, there were just some intimate details I couldn't leave out. They were reflective of the insanity I was living in and the hell I was putting myself through. I understand that I in no way have to share the things I am about to share with you. But I want to. For better or worse.

So, if you are in any way sensitive to explicit references about self-harm, eating disorders, bullying, alcohol abuse, sexual assault and mental health, I would put this book down.

For those of you who want to carry on with this collection of confessions, please believe me when I say everything works out in the end. I think.

This is my confessional…

Confessional.

There's a secret on the tip of my tongue
and it's burning a hole between my lungs
There's no grace for what e have done
but e must face what l've become

Hiding six feet under has always been my way
and though the honesty hurts, the lying was worse
Can't take this to the grave....

This is my confessional
of things that l have buried low
This is my confessional
Please will you redeem my soul.

Holy water on the tip of my tongue there's
so much sin for just 21
Hear my penance and all l have done
this self destructive war l've won.
l've come out from under to die another day
And though the honesty hurts the crying
was worse now tell me l'll be saved

Throw stones if you want to
Break bones if you want to
that high horse have a good view?
l confess.

Chapter One

CONFESSIONAL

There are many things I must clarify before I start. Firstly, and most importantly, it is far too easy to blame parents when it comes to the realms of a child with addiction problems. Here and now, I'm stating for the record that I had a gloriously happy childhood. I never wanted for anything. My parents, Patricia and Aquinas, made countless sacrifices to ensure that I received every best opportunity this world has to offer. Not only that, they gave me all the love I could ever need.

Neither of my parents drank heavily or gambled with their lives in any way. They took my brothers – Jason, Gavin and Aaron – and me to church every weekend and ensured we spent quality time together as a family. They allowed me to pursue every hobby I ever wanted, provided private tuition when necessary and gave me the freedom to make my own decisions and allowed me to grow into my own person.

With all these blessings, neither of them could have prevented or have been prepared for me and my upside down brain. I had a very sheltered upbringing and for this I'm very thankful. This may appear as though I'm boasting about how swell my childhood and upbringing were, but I'm just trying to express my gratitude to my parents for giving me the best start in life. I am loved and I love them.

Another preconceived idea that I wish to pre-emptively squash, before anyone suggests otherwise, is that my mental state throughout my teenage years was a consequence of my television appearance on *The X Factor* in 2011, at the age of 16. It would be simple to admit this as the truth, but it is not. My addictions were not a product of the show; my mental constitution was on a downhill trajectory long before – as you will come to learn. I had been held in the arms of addictive and self-destructive behaviour many years prior. As much as I would like to use the excuse of 'child star' as the catalyst to my issues, I can't. Truth be told, there is no one factor, moment or event in my life on which I can blame my past behaviour. Obviously, this leaves me with more questions than answers. I have always just been this way and it is of no fault of anyone else's actions nor my own.

An assumption, I find – spoken publicly by those who have never met me – is that my alcohol addiction is a by-product of the career path I have chosen. People have a false narrative of what the music industry is like. That the documentation of 'sex, drugs and rock'n'roll' means this portrayal is true of everyone in the job.

That the 'industry' is riddled with only temptation and that it's almost a rite of passage to fall victim to the nature of it all. Trust me, this isn't true. Though I am an addict, my working environment never fed my issues. I was lucky enough to surround myself – not through choice but sheer luck – with people who never did anything to excess. There were never any crazy after parties, no hangers-on offering me drugs or any sexual bartering for success. I know this may be true for some but thankfully that is not my story. No one ever pacified my destruction. I was only ever surrounded by people who wanted to help and ensure that I was as well as I could be. My management have had to pull me back from the edge of the ledge on numerous occasions – but only to rescue me from myself. There have been many times that I wanted to jump out of the burning building that was my life but I was literally saved by my team, friends and family, fire fighting on my behalf, even when I would often reject their lifelines. If it weren't for their love and support, I would not be here today. So, before you read on and potentially attempt to blame those around me, know that there is no sole cause or person to point the finger at. For years I pointed the finger at myself and that merely fed into a vicious cycle of self-hatred and justifications for how I could treat myself so badly. For years I truly believed I was a vile and horrible person who did not deserve any good in my life. That doesn't make me a bad person, I know that now. I'm just a human being who made bad choices.

For the last few years, I have felt as though I have been living a lie. Or a double life at least. For when I tell people I don't drink, smoke, do drugs or sleep around they think that this is me being a

very cautious adult. When the truth is, it's from learning that I can't do those things. That my internal reward system is wired the other way around to most 'normal' people and that's just the way I am. Marry this with cripplingly low self-esteem and social anxiety and you have a recipe for disaster. I understand that I in no way have to share the things I am about to share with you, but I want to. And I have wanted to for a long time. It is only now, with the release of *Confessional*, an album of which I am incredibly proud, and one that defines me as an artist, that I am ready for my fans to know all of the secrets I possess. The weight that has been lifted just from writing down my life is something I'll never fully be able to explain. To know that after this, I can openly talk about these issues I have kept hidden for so long, is truly freeing. For without the events that I have gone through in my life, I wouldn't be the person I am today. The person I once couldn't even look at in a mirror but can now love to the best of my ability. Trying my best to never take my life for granted when I almost lost it so many times. I'm one of the lucky ones and though none of us make it out of this life alive, I know that I've tried my hardest to live the best life I possibly can. To try and be present. To be a good daughter, a good friend and a good person. I may have lost myself countless times along the way, but I am finally the me I was always supposed to be.

I hope this book – these confessions, my life – reads as frank, and is as fascinating to read as it has been to live it.

So Cold

I miss you more and more each day
I'd let you know but you're not around to say
I miss you like I miss my youth
but gone are those days too

You left me without a warning, you left me without a word
You left me now I'm mourning the goodbye I never heard

I'd still sleep with the lights on, but I don't sleep anymore
I'd still sleep with the lights on, but I don't sleep
now you're gone....

You're too young to be sad they say
You're too young to be. So cold
You're too young to be sad they say
You're too young to be so old

The doctor says I'll feel no pain but colours fade
turning all my blues to grey. I miss you like
I miss my home. But it's gone now that I'm
grown. Now all that's left are the melodies
from a song I'll never play. So I bathe inside
these memories. Before the numb takes them away

Chapter Two

SO COLD

There are certain things we inherit from our families. Maybe a facial feature, hair colour or even just a surname. Those little things I used to hate about myself I now embrace. I have my father's eyes and my mother's face. Features I now cherish. For, now that I live far away in London, I only have to look in the mirror to be reminded of where I came from.

However, there are some things I've inherited in my blood that I've had to make peace with: my depression, and struggle for mental health, is an illness that runs in my family.

Though, rarely discussed, my family's issues with mental health run deep on both sides for generations. My insomnia was a birthday gift from my mother's side of the family and my addictive nature from my father's. Though I struggle with both daily, even today, it softens the blow to know that I've never been alone. It's just the hand I've been dealt; I'm lucky enough that both of these issues are manageable with time and practice.

I grew up in Gortin, County Tyrone, Northern Ireland, and was lucky that both my parents worked full time jobs. Even though we were by no means rich, they always ensured we had everything we needed and more. This, however, was not enough to deprogramme the negative voices that have resided in my head since. Even though my childhood was filled with moments of pure happiness, the demons were never far behind. For as long as I can remember, I've always felt a powerful internal sense of 'less than enough' – a concept that even I struggle to describe out loud. It's just a feeling of constant guilt I struggle to shake. When bad things would happen, I would blame myself. Always. To do that requires a massive ego, which is something I, paradoxically, have forever possessed, but it was frail and powered by low self-esteem. The worst concoction. I don't recall a time when I wasn't overwhelmingly insecure about something. I think it all stems from my fear of being perceived as unintelligent. Sounds stupid, right? I know I'm not a genius with a high IQ, but for some reason I am crippled by others thinking I am not clever. These feelings of intellectual inadequacy started back when I was at school and my failure to find solace in education and struggle to keep up with my classmates. My defects all started here.

Unlike the rest of my family, I attended a Gaelic-speaking playschool and primary school, close to where my parents lived. After school, I attended private tuition for all subjects, including learning to speak and read English too, so as not to fall behind.

When I was seven my mother withdrew me from primary school. It was becoming difficult for her to help me with my homework when she didn't speak Irish herself. I didn't mind the move since I knew lots of girls in the English speaking school; both buildings were located on the same campus. I remember my first day as if it were yesterday. I was stood outside the classroom with a teaching assistant, terrified as she explained again what was happening. "Look for the desk with your name on and just sit down, you'll be all right," she reassured me. I wandered in, looking for the name tags on the table and I sat down. Turns out, it wasn't my seat at all. In my nervous hurry to sit, I accidentally took the seat of a Joanna and not Janet. Joanna politely pointed to where my seat was. Not before my face went beetroot with embarrassment. It was in that classroom that I first began to be treated differently from my peers. Though I was never tested on my learning abilities, my teacher gave me different homework and separate worksheets from those of my classmates. I was too young to know why but not young enough not to feel the isolation. As the years went on in that school, the differences became more apparent. While my classmates were doing multiplication, I was doing addition. My reading material was different too. The only time I wasn't treated differently was during playtime, when my classmates treated me the same. During one class, myself and three others were taken to the side of the classroom. I would come to learn that we were in the 'Special Learners' group. Academically, I was more than a year behind everyone else. I didn't feel stupid – nor did I feel challenged or pushed.

One of the main problems that contributed to my frustrations was that I'd already learnt a lot of what my classmates were being taught but I had done so with my private tutor. It was music, of course, that allowed my mother to withdraw me from the school without feeling any sense of wrongdoing. The government had just commenced an initiative to allow four children from each year the chance to learn violin. When I heard the news, I was over the moon. I'd already been learning how to play the fiddle outside of school time so the prospect of pursuing it at school gave me a buzz. Unfortunately, unlike the other schools involved in the programme there was no test. The four pupils were picked out by our teacher and not by the results of an auditory exam. I was heartbroken. When I came home that evening I cried to my mother. I was distraught from not being chosen. Music had become the only thing I believed I truly excelled at ever since I was three years old when I stole a tin whistle off of my brother. Music had become, very quickly, a huge grounding influence in my young life. So, to not even have been considered for the programme hurt the feelings of my eight-year-old self. I had been rejected, perhaps for the first time, for something I deemed incredibly important. When my mother heard the news, she was furious. Not that I hadn't been picked but because I hadn't even been considered. She suspected favouritism because I had fallen behind in other subjects. She called up the school demanding answers. When they failed to pacify her with any, she decided to withdraw me from that school. My brother would be joining me too. With that, we attended a primary school in Plumbridge, a neighbouring village. We didn't even wait until the end of year to move. It was immediate. My brother wasn't at all happy. It seemed unfair to him to have to leave all his friends behind over something he didn't understand.

My first few days at the new school were rough. Being the new kid is hard, it's a feeling you never forget. Everyone there knew each other. I knew no one. My Mum decided not to tell my new school that I was a 'special learner' too, so I was thrown in at the deep end with my studies. I think my mother didn't want to believe I was 'special'. I was overwhelmed. My classmates were already practicing multiplication and division. I couldn't say anything to my teacher. I kept my head down and tried my best to make sense of it all. It was a tough few weeks but I found my feet and

eventually flourished. I found myself on the same level as my peers quicker than anyone could've anticipated. I blossomed socially, too, and made friends. My memories from that school are only positive, and when I think back to those times, I smile. After just a few weeks, my teacher announced to the class that we'd be having a music exam. The same exam that was denied at my previous school. Not long after, an external instructor came to our class and gave us the exam, which effectively meant playing a CD that spoke questions. Nothing difficult, just, "Which note is higher?" and "What instrument is this?" When the results came back, the teacher announced that I had been accepted onto the programme; I was to learn classical violin after all. I couldn't have been happier. The whole experience of struggling at my first school to finally being allowed to learn an instrument I was passionate about, really had a big impact on me. I still remember the frustration and anxiety of feeling left out, rejected, and the effect it had on me. Every time I pick up a violin now, an intense wave of emotion hits me. If the tin whistle was the door that opened up my love of music, learning to play the violin was my way in.

Different by Default

Hate is a strong word, isn't it? It's loaded with such anger. But, sadly, I honestly don't remember a time in my life when I didn't hate myself. It's often assumed that such strong feelings would come solely from my exterior appearance but that's not my truth. I've always been highly critical of myself across all elements. As I

would soon come to learn, I am an all-rounder when it comes to self-loathing. I find the voice in my head almost unbearable and always have. I just assumed that because I couldn't stand me, then surely everyone else felt the same. I felt as though I was the pity friend. The one people let hang around because they are too kind not to leave them on their own. Maybe it's due to being the final child of four. Having three older brothers and being the only girl, I was different by default. It always felt as though I never truly fitted in anywhere. This became more apparent as I transitioned from primary to secondary school. The kids in my class all seemed to hail from the local town. I didn't. The kids all had short and uniformed hair, even the girls. I didn't. My parents had refused to let me colour or cut my hair. *Ever*. This meant I had blonde hair down to my hips. It was permanently frizzy. Neither my mother nor I knew what to do with it, so she made the mistake of brushing it in the mornings. If you are cursed/blessed with curly hair, you'll know this is possibly the worst thing to do with it because it doubles in size, frizzes up and has no curl definition. I was a walking fluff ball (still am!). This wasn't the only feature of my appearance that made me stand out. My crooked teeth seemed to point everywhere except up. On the bus home from school one of the first days, a girl announced out loud that I was the "Caucasian *Ugly Betty*". My braces gave it away. Perhaps she was right, I thought.

So began the playground bullying that would torment me for the next three years. Though nothing they said ever really hurt me; it could never compare to the vile things I called myself in my head on a daily basis. All their taunts did was to re-affirm (in my head) that I deserved to be treated the way I treated myself. With the onset of adolescence, puberty and my teens, I could find my inner monologue become even more cruel and to the point. I became more depressed and isolated. I found myself unable to make friends. Even those I did consider friends at the time would join in when the insults flew around the classroom. Isolation became protection. By 11, I had descended into a deep state of depression. My newfound hormones, mixed with desolation anxiety, left me deflated a lot. At 12, I was self-harming. It seemed logical to me, the next obvious step. I deserved the pain. I'd become so numb that I needed to feel something, even if it was excruciating pain. *Especially* if it was excruciating pain. It made me feel human again. It was a fleeting habit, this time, gone by the summer of my third year at secondary school. But it would return with greater frequency and force, as you will discover.

Everything's Changing

I was always an active child, happy playing in the great outdoors, but now something had… *changed*. That summer, aged 13, I locked myself away. My sleeping pattern was off the rails. I'd go to bed at 6 a.m. and wake up at 4 p.m. Some days, to my mother's disgust, she'd wake me up at 5.30 p.m., when she came back from work. When I wasn't asleep, I was in bed with my laptop. I found a website that allowed me to be someone else. It was a social media site where you could create a character and interact with people all over the world. Automatically, I felt less alone and less isolated.

This website, though innocent, quickly led to addictive behaviour. Hours would merge into days with very few breaks. I would tear myself away only to eat. Beyond my obsession with the internet, and writing songs, which had begun to develop out of my love of learning to play the guitar, and singing at the same time, I didn't have much interest in doing anything at all. Even on a bright summer's day, all I felt was the grey abyss swallowing me whole. My love of the great outdoors had become less great. This feeling never seemed to pass. For years it felt like the only constant I could rely on. I still managed to have moments of fun during my early teenage years, of course, but I was always greeted by the black dog at the beginning and end of the day. I would often cry myself to sleep. In some regards I wasn't altogether upset. When I watched interviews on YouTube with my favourite musicians, they all seemed to be haunted too. The sadness allowed me to write music that meant something to me. The lyrics would usually come first, beginning life as a poem that I'd write in the small hours of the morning. Some would later become lyrics in tracks from my first album, *Hide & Seek*, and others remain locked in my diary, secrets forever sealed.

By my mid-teens, I'd finally made friends, true friends who could accept me for who I was. Scars and all. These friends helped me balance out my sadness with real joy, and I am forever thankful to have found them. Who knows what may have happened if I hadn't?

By the time I was 15, I was still riddled with voices, self-loathing and depression, but I never let it stop me. I could never bare to let it win. I continued to pursue my school work and still managed to achieve above average grades. I even started to compete in local singing competitions (Taylor Swift's 'White Horse' and Vanessa Carlton's 'A Thousand Miles' were my go-to songs), playing open mic acoustic nights at a local pub, where people would applaud quietly. This was also around the time I began to upload cover songs to YouTube – Florence and the Machine's 'Cosmic Love' was the first. My music, and the music of artists who I adored, was my lighthouse at the centre of a dark sea. Though, I never thought at the age of 15 that I'd pursue songwriting as a career. That idea was a dream too far for a girl from Gortin. Instead, I opted to learn the drums. I was desperate to write songs and be in a band, but not have to be the face of it all… I was too self-conscious. The entire reason I began entering singing competitions wasn't so that I could pursue singing, it was to earn enough money to buy a drum kit of my own! My YouTube videos had also started to do well, with people from all over the world watching them. I even had classmates and locals complimenting me about how good they thought they were. I thought they were taking the piss out of me.

By the time I turned 16, my cover of Elton John's 'Your Song' had started to get significant hits and nice comments, so much so that my Mum submitted the video to *The X Factor* 2011. Despite being riddled with internal nerves, self-doubt and uncertainty about whether it was the right path for me, I decided to go for it. I made it to the live show stages of the series. A dream for any contestant.

As it turned out, I spent more time in bathrooms having panic attacks. Instead of having the time of my life, performing songs to millions of people every week, I wanted to beat my own brain.

I often wondered how many contestants had felt the same as me, crying in the bathrooms at Wembley Stadium, terrified to go on stage, crippled by self-loathing.

During my time on the show the dark clouds came back in full force. If I wasn't rehearsing a performance or surrounded by other contestants at the *X Factor* house, I would be contemplating suicide, though I could never bring myself to think that word. I would daydream of how I would do it, when I would do it and what I would write in my farewell. One day, I got close. I had a moment of insanity, but I snapped myself back from the brink. I can't tell you how. Something had to be done. I spoke to the crew on the show. To my surprise, I was reassured that I wasn't the only one going through it. That other contestants had been visiting a therapist and psychologist too. The day after, I was taken to London's Harley Street for an assessment. After an extensive written Q&A about my mental health, the doctor was given my answers. After waiting for what seemed an eternity, the doctor ushered me into the consultation room. She told me the results. On a scale of 1–100, 100 being the worst, I scored 93. This was not good news. Proof, were it needed, of just how on the edge of suicide I was. With my prescription in hand, I was then sent downstairs to see the psychologist. "So, Janet, tell me about you? How're you feeling?" she said. I broke down. I begin bawling my eyes out. It had been so long since anyone had actually asked me how I was. It overwhelmed me and I couldn't get the words out. For months I'd put on a brave face for the cameras but the truth was, I was broken. No one around me even cared enough to ask if I was all right. So long as I was ready for the performance, that's all that mattered. Eventually, I ended up telling my handler (a person hired by the show to assist the contestants) that I wanted to leave the show. I knew that word travelled very quickly behind the scenes. It was a week after I'd started taking Prozac, prescribed to me by the doctor. Despite being voted first for the first five weeks of the show, I was eliminated in week eight after a "terrible" performance. After I was out, I was offered a place on the *X Factor* tour. I agreed. I'd hoped that this would be the end of the sadness. That is not the way the world works. I gave up on the Prozac. I didn't know what was worse: to feel everything all at once or to feel nothing at all. I opted for the latter. The medication robbed me of my ability to express myself creatively. My songwriting felt forced and the lyrics disingenuous. I began to use alcohol as a replacement for the medication, but nothing worked. The waves kept crashing.

I was on and off anti-depressants for the duration of my explosive drinking period between the ages of 18 and 20. Obviously, they were never going to work since I was consuming booze at an unhealthy rate – but it distracted me, at least, from the voices in my head. They were drunk too.

It wasn't until two years of sobriety, at the age of 22, that I felt my mental health issues return. At that point, I tried to write this book and a 'hit song'. Neither of which I achieved. Thankfully, I was in recovery from anorexia – a process I'll discuss later in the book. In two years of being sober, I learnt how to cook nutritious meals, work out and look after my body. There was something missing though. As I wasn't acting out any of my negative behaviours by being on the bottle, my brain got bored and agitated. It was itchy and wanted to cause harm. I ended up hitting an all-time low with my depression. I know it was the lowest I've ever been because for the first time ever, I contemplated quitting music. I was truly lost. I'd been in the industry for seven years and in my eyes, I'd had no visible success. Obviously when you're depressed, nothing is right. I knew I had to find help because no amount of self-care was working. I flew home to Ireland, met with a doctor and told him the truth. It wasn't a decision I took lightly. I didn't want to go back on medication but I didn't want to die either. I was exhausted from thinking about suicide all the time. How much can one person dream about their own demise? I began taking Prozac again. It worked. I felt emotionally stable. The downside was I'd apparently lost my mojo for music. By the second month, I was exhausted from hearing from my team that I'd "lost my spark" and wasn't being productive enough. My music and my writing were suffering. It became too much. "If they want to see me suicidal again, then fuck it," I thought. Against doctor's orders, I stopped taking the medication. The darkness returned and so did the desire to drown. But without the drugs dulling my senses, my passion for music returned. I began working with producer Jonathan Quarmby. Over a period of several months, we wrote some great songs together and I knew right away that I wanted him to produce my second record. I had my drive back. I was able to put my head back into my music and I became excited at the thought of recording my songs. When the sadness came, I transformed it to poetry. I used my negative thoughts for good. When I felt joy, I made music. I may have been unstable but at least I was creating something I believed in.

Hello My Old Friend

For five years, my depression would ebb and flow. But in winter 2018 the darkness came back to haunt me. My second album was not progressing as quickly as I wanted it to. I was working as hard as I could muster, but nothing seemed to be coming to fruition at the pace I needed. I was burning out and my passion for music was flickering. I again started to question my place in the music industry. I'd hit one too many bumps in the road, as you'll read in the coming chapters, and I began disengaging. I had logged out from life. I wasn't fully aware of when it happened; one day I just realised I wasn't here. Through the years, I've experienced mini episodes of depersonalisation and derealisation. The trouble with these states is that, more often than not, you're unaware that it's happening. It's also something that, unless you've experienced it before, it's incredibly difficult to explain. It's as if you're on autopilot. You can still function completely and get things done, just do so without being present or feeling anything about it. I didn't cry. I didn't laugh. I just flatlined. All I saw was grey. I constantly asked myself questions "Who even am I?" and "Is this all there is?" Beyond the album delays, nothing in my life could warrant me feeling such a way. I had a social life, I was dating someone I liked and I even had a song – 'I Lied to You' – being released. But none of this even penetrated the surface. From emails to appointments, I couldn't remember anything. Some days I would wake up and, for a few seconds, forget who I was, where I was; struggling to remember what my mother's face looked like. None of this was alarming enough for me to do anything about apparently, so I floated on.

By December 2018, I was drinking and using sleep medication heavily again and by January 2019 I was in rehab. I called my manager Rick and said, "See you when I feel better". I just left. I'd officially lost my marbles. Again. One minute I'd want to hang myself off a ceiling beam and the next I was laughing at a joke someone was telling. I was incredibly unstable. After two weeks spent in solo and group therapy, I finally got a rein on my emotions again. I realised that my wayward mind is only uncontrollable when I don't deal with what I'm feeling. It was a mini revelation. I had to confront my demons, not run away with them. After a month, I left rehab. I knew what I needed to do: I got a new therapist in London, close to where I was living. I took the first step of getting help on a weekly basis. It's easy to fall apart if you're in pieces. I don't ever intend on letting things get that bad ever again. I want to be present in my life.

Holding onto Waves

Though my feelings of intense sadness still pulse around my body, I'm much more accepting of them. For me, the key to handling depression is accepting it's there, realising it may always be there, and recognising that it's not your fault and allowing yourself to not feel angry at yourself over it. The world has yet to catch up with accepting mental illness without prejudice. I realised that it was OK to stay in bed all day, if that's what I felt would get me through the day. Having a depression that doesn't go away teaches you how to cope with it and allows you to become familiar with your own limitations. I know if my room gets messy, my brain is messy. If I haven't had a one-to-one with someone in two days, I need to socialise. These are just two of my own markers, but we all have our own. Mental health is just as important as physical health. My struggle for mental health will stay with me forever, but all I can do is hold onto the waves when they hit the shore.

Saint of the Sinners

I'm on my hands and knees again
Singing a symphony of sins.
I'm crying, I'm crying again
And I am sorry for what I've done
apologies from empty lungs
I'm lying, I'm lying again

You let me drown in holy water, you let me fall on holy ground
I spent my life at your altar, but all you did was hold me down

Cause I'm the saint of the sinners I'm the saint of the sinners
Don't trust a word I say and don't take my crown away
'cause I'm the saint of the sinners.

I'd say I'd see you in the end but I
Can't consider you a friend
I'm screaming, I'm screaming again
You buried me with no Amen
So one day there would be revenge
I'm singing, I'm singing again...

I am more than the tears I've cried. I am more than the
blood that's dried. I am more than my tiger stripes.
I am more than the sharpest lives. And I know that
this lightening strikes, lightening strikes twice....

Chapter Three

SAINT OF THE SINNERS

I was 12 years old when I first discovered the relief of silver upon my skin. I had become a self-harmer, a cutter, a consequence of a mind filled with fear. Long sleeves soon became my fashion of choice, even in the middle of a July heatwave. In all honesty, when I first discovered a pair of rusty scissors in the downstairs bathroom I never fully considered the ramifications of what I'd carry around on my skin for an eternity.

I remember everything, except the reason why. Why did I think slicing my skin would be the most efficient painkiller? Was this behaviour learned? If so, where? What hurt me so much that it drove me to this? But there I sat on the floor of the shower, cross-legged, limp-wristed and emotionally numb. Here I was, a school kid, barely old enough to be allowed to go to the local shop on my own, cutting myself to feel alive. It never seemed to fully soothe the pain that I didn't completely comprehend. Thankfully, this form of self-destruction didn't last long. I put the scissors down after a friend of mine discovered the scars – wounds – hidden beneath my sweater. Pinky promises were made that I would never break the borders of my body again. Sadly, I would break this vow seven years later, at 19. I would be found clutching my dark red-stained thigh in one hand, being transported to A&E at 3 a.m. That would be the last time. But allow me to rewind…

"Why hast thou made me thus?"

"Red sky at night, a shepherd's delight," my father's voice resounded in my mind. On any evening we caught the sunset together, he would always paraphrase this bible verse of Matthew. We'd often watch the sunset roll over the Sperrin Mountains from our garden. I'd sit atop the concrete pillars at the base of my parents' front field. My Dad's hands were always there, propping me up, ensuring I did not fall. It was in those fields of home that the fondest memories of my childhood occurred. It was 1998 (I was four), and uncharacteristically warm for an Irish summer. Because both my parents worked, my brothers and I required babysitters for the summer school holidays. My cousins, Donna and Laura, were gainfully employed. They lived a mile and a half away, in the village of Rousky. They were both in their teens and, in my eyes, they were the pinnacle of all things 'cool'. On the days when they'd look after us, we were seldom indoors. We'd spend hours playing games like 40/40, hide-and-seek and squash. On particularly hot days, we could be found on the roof of the toy shed, sunbathing. They both created such joy out of the ordinary. Once they found a pot of paint that was left over from when my father redecorated the house. They painted their feet and walked around the roof. When I awoke from my sunbathing snooze, I was delighted to see a 'fairy' had visited me in my sleep, so they told me. My youth was magical.

But even in those sunny days, shadows of the mind were still being cast. I possessed an insidious voice of self-loathing. It was rare that it would rear its head and, as a child, I assumed it was normal. It was around this time that I first recall hurting myself. In the early twilight hours of that summer, the laughter of children carried through the brushes. My babysitters, brothers and myself could be found climbing on top of the large, round hay bales of the season's yield. It was rare that my parents enforced any rules or stipulations to our fun but this time they told us, "no playing on the bales." We'd been well warned against using the bales as climbing frames. This was just enough warning to tease the desire of discovery in six children. We proceeded to disobey my parents' order and instead opted for pinky promises that we wouldn't tell them that we had. No one wanted to get in trouble. We clambered on top of the bales and made the jump of a few feet between each. It was a life-size version of leap frog. It didn't take long for my small body to become tired from the exertion. I'd made one jump too many and as I attempted to leap I instead collided face first with the top of the bale. As I slid down the bale and my head hit the floor, I could hear the gasps from the others. The pain would have been agonising if it were not for the embarrassment. When I smacked the floor, I was simultaneously hit by an overwhelming sense of fear – not for my own safety, but for the ramifications for Donna and Laura. What was to happen to them if my parents knew I fell playing on the bales? What would happen if they knew that we defied their command? I didn't care for the pain, *I cared for them.* I didn't want everyone to get in trouble for my own stupidity. So, I ran. I ran into the house and into my room. With my eyes enveloped in tears I began screaming between fractured breaths. "Why God? Why? How could you let me be so stupid?" I closed my fists and I began to punch myself in the stomach. With all my might I hit myself over and over again. I couldn't cope with the guilt. It was already eating me up on the inside because in my mind, everyone was to suffer for my idiocy. My incompetence. I made my way to the mirror and wiped the tears from my eyes. I stared intently at my reflection and I yelled at myself. The cruel thoughts that usually floated inaudibly around my head, I said them aloud with venomous intent. Never breaking eye contact. When I finally tired myself out, I slid down the wall, utterly defeated. I crawled into a ball and I closed my eyes, hoping to escape my reality. I must've fallen asleep then, for this is when my memory of that night ends.

From that moment on, the destructive voice never left my head. I never grew out of it. In fact, I grew into it. As I crept my way into adolescence, that's when the monsters came out to play. They were being aided by the taunting words of fellow classmates. Their insults justified the negative emotions I was harbouring towards

myself. They gave me the false rationale to hate myself even more. The words of others solidified that I was indeed a terrible human being. I deserved to be punished. The bullying never stopped, because I never let it. I was depressed, at 11. The insults were evolving with me.

The bullying only became a daily thing in my life when I went to secondary school. I was a very easy target. If it wasn't the frizzy waist-length blonde hair, it was my crooked teeth or the fact that I was more interested in horses than people. The more I started to find and express myself, the more I'd get picked on. I was the happiest when I was listening to or writing sad songs. I was into rock music – bands like Paramore, My Chemical Romance and Bring Me the Horizon. At the time it was all that I would listen to. In the days before I had an MP3 player, I'd wake up early to watch the heavy rock music on rotation on music TV channels. I would wear black skinny jeans, Converse trainers and band T-shirts. My wardrobe wouldn't have been complete without my staple diet of plaid shirts. Nowadays, none of those things are out of place and it would be absurd to mock someone over such clothing choices. But in the town where I grew up, appearance alone was enough to be picked on every day. In 2005, no one had even begun wearing skinny jeans in my town. The internet had yet to take over teenagers' lives so 'alternative styles' were not a thing where I lived. You were just 'different', and that was bad. The kids in my class would rarely call me by my name; I was labelled the 'emo' kid. The term itself is harmless these days but it wasn't back then. Now don't get me wrong, I was an emo kid and I was OK with that.

What wasn't OK was my class mates telling me to "kill myself" or "to go and slit my wrists". What's even funnier about this is that I didn't slit my wrists at the time as they commanded – that would happen months later, at my own request. So back then I'd roll up my sleeves and show them my unscathed wrists. I don't even think the bullying was the worst part; it was the bystanders that let it happen – the teachers. They could hear what my classmates were saying but they chose to ignore it.

One day the bullying became physical. I was outside of my friends' form class, chatting with her before the bell rang. Out of nowhere, and with no warning, one of the boys (who was over six-foot tall and of muscular build) picked me up and threw me across the hallway. In an almost comedic fashion, my back and arm hit the thick fire door and then I slid down. I laughed when I hit the ground. I was in shock. Moments later I realised that my arm was incredibly sore. I ended up having to get my Dad to come pick me up and take me to A&E. My head of year simply told me that he "obviously had a crush on me, he just doesn't know how to express it". If things couldn't get any worse, the boy turned up to my house that night, out of the blue, with his Dad. That night, I bore witness to the most awkward apology ever.

The internet and social media were such new things when I was growing up, that real rules hadn't been made yet. It was the Wild West when it came to being mean and offensive. Nothing was policed and there were no repercussions for what you said online. In my early teens/preteens, Bebo was the place to be. It was basically Facebook but more custom. Beyond the amount of horrible wall posts people would leave there was a new feature added: 'band pages'. Innocent enough if you have a band and want to share your music. Not innocent when people make hate pages about you under the 'band' tab. This allowed the members to remain private but they could invite all their friends. Perfect. Who doesn't want to see 100 people like your hate page? Eventually, I stopped taking the bus home from school. I didn't feel safe being picked on by people who lived so close.

When my school day was done I'd always go to my mother's workplace and sit in the kitchen. I would peacefully do my homework, read or listen to music. I probably should've been more upset by the inconvenience of losing two hours of my day but I actually liked it there. The women who worked with my mother were always so lovely to me. They treated me so well and would always ask me questions. It was oddly comforting to be surrounded by adults, probably because they were less judgemental than my classmates. Also, I was always content whenever my Mum was near. She was, and is, a human comfort blanket. Regrettably, I never told my family about the school bullies. They were incomparable to the real bully who lived in my head. I needed to confront her first.

Things got easier when I finally made friends. By 15 I had made three friends – Megan, Rachel A and Rachel C – still my best friends today. When you're not a lone wolf, the bullying relents. Or so I thought. My life drastically changed overnight when my audition on *The X Factor* aired. My name was all over the nationwide and regional press, blog posts and the internet. In the beginning, I couldn't keep up with all the comments so I barely read them. When I did stumble upon negative responses online, I found it easy to brush them off. It was as though I was almost too busy to take the hate personally. Or it was nothing in comparison to the negative voices that floated around my own head. Fast-forward to a year after the show and things had begun to change. My self-worth was at an all-time low and I was trying to keep people interested in myself and my album project. This meant more time on social media, which meant more time reading comments. I quickly began using the mean comments as justification for my self-hatred. If I was feeling insecure about my weight, I'd seek out hateful comments about it, or whatever I disliked about myself that day. It was easy to believe it. The more I allowed the hate in, the more I ignored the positive. I remember once even posting a photo for an anti-suicide campaign and reading comments from people detailing why – and how – I should kill myself.

I can't ignore the face-to-face, as well as behind my back, bullying that occurred after my time on the show. When I'd come home to visit my friends and family from time to time, I couldn't walk down the street without people yelling abuse from their cars or having people point and laugh at me. I would think it paranoia if it weren't mentioned by the people I was with. I'd try to have a few quiet drinks in a pub with my friends but would have strangers coming up and telling me all the reasons why they didn't like me. Once, on a night out in my local town, I even had a girl hurl abuse at me and later throw a punch at me – all because I was just being myself. I felt as though I couldn't escape the negativity. I wasn't safe online and I wasn't safe in real life. It got to the point where I stopped leaving the house all together.

The First Cut

By 12, I had turned into an emotional ghost. I wanted so much to feel something but the numbness always won. I couldn't take it anymore. So, one evening, I did something I thought I was physically incapable of doing. I don't know how I came to the conclusion that this would be a good solution to my situation, but there I was – grabbing a pair of kitchen scissors, rusted by age and neglect, on my way to the bathroom. I hid them in a towel so no one would see. I had thought my actions through.

The bathroom was minuscule. There was just enough room for a toilet and a shower. I turned the water on, to conceal my wincing. I took off my top and sat down on the shower floor, armed with the rusty scissors. I didn't even question what came next. I eyed up my arm, plotting where to start. I unfolded the scissors, clenched my left fist and started cutting. It didn't take long before I got frustrated. The rusty scissors weren't doing the job I'd hoped they would. It took a lot of force to even draw a scratch, never mind bleed. I stepped out of the shower. I was angry, at myself and at the inanimate object in my hands. "How could I be so terrible at this too?" I wondered to myself. I sat there on the floor, soaking wet, crouched over, trying to make deeper cuts. I had to stop, I was physically exhausted from the effort it took to bleed. Not one tear fell from my eyes. When the endorphins kicked in that's when

I finally felt something. It was the sweet release of relief. For the first time in what felt like forever I didn't feel numb. I sat there in awe of the blood trickling down my arm. "Is this what it is?" I thought, "Is this all it is to be human?" In those moments, all that mattered was feeling pain. In the days that followed, I lived in fear of someone finding out. I didn't care that I was slicing my skin for relief, but I did care if someone were to find out.

I covered my arms with bracelets that I'd acquired over the years. No one thinks twice if a teenage girl wears an excessive amount of bangles. My school uniform was an aid to my veil too. There was only one downside. The wool from my school jumper made the scabs itchy, but I deserved the discomfort, I would tell myself. In the following weeks I experimented with different instruments to better self-harm. It didn't matter what weapon I chose, none seemed to fully pacify my needs. Each time I would sneak into the bathroom, I left unfulfilled. When I first began to cut, I'd only do it when I felt incredibly depersonalised. I used it as more of an alarm clock, hoping it would be a reality wake-up call. I never thought much of it...

... until the day I got caught.

Hurts Like Heaven

The likelihood of getting found out was slim. Or so I thought. No one had seen me unclothed since I was a child, not even my parents. In PE class I would always get changed in a cubicle or hide in the bathrooms until everyone was gone. It was uncommon anyone would see my forearms because, living in Ireland, we rarely had the weather for it.

One day the sun decided to bless us with its presence. Instead of being overjoyed like the rest of my classmates, I found myself sweating with fear. I couldn't take my school jumper off; people – *teachers* – would see the wounds, cut fresh the night before. I could feel the polyester jumper rubbing against the cuts. The sweat made them sting and the sleeves made them itchy. During my science lesson, I could feel my irritability rising. I was on the brink of tears. It was a mixture of pain, shame and guilt. My best friend, Megan, asked me if I was all right. She could sense something wasn't. Exasperated, I raised my hand and waited to be noticed by the teacher. With my arm in the air I reassured Megan that I was OK, I just needed to use the bathroom. I was excused and I hurried out of the classroom into the nearest bathroom. Frantically, I checked every stall, ensuring no one was there. Satisfied that I was alone, I slid my jumper off. I removed the many bracelets I was wearing and began running my arm under the cold water. As much as it stung, it didn't hurt nearly as much as it did before. The relief was short lived. The door opened to the bathroom. I froze. Like a deer in the headlights. I yelled at my brain to tell my feet to move, but there I stood. As the door opened I locked eyes with Megan. I was more afraid of her than I would've been a teacher. Before I had the time to hide my arm, it was too late. The eye contact had already been broken and her gaze had fallen upon that of the marks. "I'm sorry," I whispered. She rushed over and hugged me. I had to explain, but the words wouldn't form. I never rehearsed what I'd say to someone if they asked me about it. I never thought anyone would see them. "It's nothing, I swear! I know this looks bad but I'm never going to do it again!" When I said it, I meant it. Megan could see it in my eyes that I wasn't lying. With the pressure of getting caught skipping class, we talked things out pretty quickly. As we walked back to the classroom I answered all her questions, but it became clear pretty quickly that I didn't really know why I was doing it. I just did. I tried explaining the relief it bought but it wasn't working. Megan finding out was the wake-up call I needed. I realised just how stupid it was to hurt myself to feel better. Cutting was the temporary fix to a much larger problem. As always, my friend refused to lay judgement. I didn't feel perhaps as much shame for doing it as maybe I would've if someone else had found out.

Outside of the classroom, I found myself bound to another pinky promise. With our fingers locked I swore that I would never cut myself again. This incident opened a dialogue that didn't exist between us yet. We'd only been friends since the start of the year and we hadn't faced any emotional tribulations up until that point. From then on, we became sisters. I never had to lie to her. I never had to hide anything because I knew that whatever secret I had, she'd keep it safe. As I have come to learn, one of my biggest flaws is that I never actually know what's eating me up until it's too late. It's as if I'm on some emotional time delay, or lag. And I found that out the hard way, and I accept that. My need to self-harm stemmed from the frustration of not feeling anything when I need to feel something, and so I never got woke to the hardest truth of the situation. Though I stayed true to my promise with Megan, I did so through a loophole. I never cut myself again while at school… but I did hurt myself by other means. When I began starving myself, I held a silent resentment against Megan. I wanted so much to pierce my skin on numerous occasions, but the fear of losing my best friend stopped me.

It wasn't until October 2013 – when, again, I felt life wasn't living up to its potential – that I broke that pinky promise. Everything had become too much again. So many things were going wrong in this period of time in my life. I found out I was bankrupt, I'd been scammed out of thousands of pounds, I despised my debut album, I loathed myself and I was feeling like a burden to everyone around me. I was emotionally desolate. Numbness isn't the absence of feelings, it's the consequence of feeling overwhelmed by too many emotions and not being able to operate. My decision to cut myself again was a reflex, triggered by the numbness. I decided one night when I was home alone that I was going to self-harm again. I was uncomfortable with how cold I was feeling about everything. My brain rationalised this decision by convincing me that I couldn't be real unless I was fully present with how I felt. After all, what's a few scars in the grand scheme of things. But, this time around, I did things differently. I didn't cut myself in the shower and I didn't use blunt scissors. I used my left hand to cut my right arm (in an act of prevention, I once got a tattoo on my left arm: as I'm right handed that was my optimum area for cutting. The deterrent didn't work). I thought it would be like the last time I'd done it – incredibly difficult to draw blood. So, I used a steak knife – great for slicing roasted meats, but not skin. When I was finished, I felt the same way I did after the first time. Frustrated with how terrible I was at it. I'd done such a poor job. I could probably have blamed the scratches on our pet cat, Ringo, and people would've believed it. This didn't stop me, however. There was something more in it that satisfied me. It made sense to reflect the chaos of my life on my arms. It quickly became more than a reality check. It became an addiction. In my head, I didn't deserve a normal body. So, I kept cutting. In the beginning, no one noticed. It was no one's business but my own. So long as it wasn't affecting my creativity or my music, I could see no reason to tell anyone.

That bubble of disillusionment eventually burst. When Rick, my manager, spotted the raw marks on my arms, my world came closing in. This was the beginning of a true dialogue about my mental health with him. It was easier to talk about my depression when we couldn't see it. When it wasn't emblazoned on my body. But, for Rick, the scars and wounds made it all real. He was incredibly understanding. More so than I believed I deserved. The initial conversation was the hardest. "Are you sure you want to do this?", "Maybe you should go home and find your head," and "What happens when the pressure – *success* – increases? Are you going to crumble?" I stood my ground. I had to articulate the only truth I know: without music, I am dead. To create is my sole purpose. Without it, I see no point in living. My brain only works in black and white, I never understood grey. I was either an artist or I wasn't living. I must've made my point clear to Rick because I wasn't sent home. We got back to work. I then knew that everyone in my team, Team JD, was coming from a loving place of concern.

When I went home that Christmas, I felt like I was being continuously watched. My brain was flooded with the constant paranoia that someone was going to catch me. Not just with the cutting, with everything. I hear it often mentioned by people in the creative industries, this fear of being 'caught out', that we're somehow frauds in our own skins. This is how I've always felt, anyway. The entire time I was home I was waiting for someone to catch me cutting, or call me out. They didn't. My mother once got close to catching me cutting. I'd just stepped out of the shower and while my hair was drying, I was running a safety pin over my wrist. My Mum knows that I'm a private person and how much I hate to be seen naked. This is how I knew her not knocking wasn't an accident. In the milliseconds it took for her to open the door, I had swooped my arm under the towel. I could see it in her face, the look of "I know you're hiding something". I was and I was doing it well. I had stocked up on black, long-sleeve leotards before my trip. I wouldn't leave my room without one on. Minus a few night time scratches with the blades of shower razors, I didn't cut myself when I was back in Ireland. I was preoccupied with the festivities of socially acceptable excessive alcohol consumption.

As the cutting got worse, the eventuality of it impacting my work did become a reality, however. During a songwriting session in Hampshire one day, I remember staying at my manager's house the night before, but neither he nor his wife was there. I was alone.

So, I wanted to get drunk, obliterated, in fact. And I wanted to tear into myself.

I made my way to the corner shop and picked up two bottles of cheap red wine. One bottle for the anaesthetic, the other for amnesia. This was the first time I'd ever mixed alcohol with self-mutilation. The pain still hit but it was muffled. This meant that I could go deeper. That I could push it just a little bit further than I had done before. In a moment of drunken destruction, I upped the stakes of my pain. I remembered the knife sharpener that lived on top of the kitchen shelf. I must have clocked it once upon a time for just that reason. Up until this point, I'd been using a knife I'd kept from my first ever apartment. It was cheap and the blade was getting dull. Trying to do any damage with it was incredibly taxing. To any sane, rational human being, the fact I got giddy over a knife sharpener would be enough to lock me up. But here I was, excited to use it. Excited to feel something sharp.

So, when I made the first swipe across my left arm, I was taken aback. It was like cutting into butter. With the mixture of Dutch courage and a fresh blade I got lost in the self-destruction. When I self-harmed, I disappeared for a little while into myself. It was as though someone else was possessing me and I would black out. At the end, I'd crash-land back into my body. My real self was left to clean up the mess (and what a mess). This instance was no exception. It could have been hours or it could have been minutes. I should have been more afraid of what I saw when I came to, but I wasn't. I was hit by the happy hormone high. I'd cut myself deeper, thicker, harder than ever before. I cleaned up the mess I'd made, the dark red blood stains showed how deep I went. I poured myself a glass of wine and kept on drinking. I never once thought about the fact that I had a writing session in the morning. I never thought of the consequences, otherwise I wouldn't have done it in the first place.

As you can imagine, the next day was sheer hell. Both my arm and my head were hung-over. This in itself is another form of self-harm. When they returned home, Rick and his wife could see what had happened. They must have just guessed, or I didn't clean up very well. I just remember the pain. They were more sympathetic than I ever deserved. But they were, quite rightly, shocked. I now had to sit in the car en route to my session with Rick. I don't remember much except for the brief toilet stop at a service station. I was in a dire need to use the bathroom for multiple reasons: one to relieve myself, another to see my reflection to ensure I was indeed alive and, lastly, to check my bandage. I knew it wasn't going to be pretty. When I touched the sleeve to pull it up, my fingers were quickly wet with blood. I had to take the bandage off. It had long forgone salvageability. I cleaned around the wound and rinsed the sleeve in the sink water. I didn't want to risk grazing my arm against anything and leaving blood stains. I didn't think about how clean the water would be or anything to do with possible infection. I just didn't want anyone to know. When I got back into the car, I assumed my position of head against the window and pretended to sleep. As much as I yearned for the real thing, I never achieved it, as my insomnia would never grace me the respite of a temporary demise. Instead, my mind was occupied with the conscious need to hold myself together.

I arrived at the session at noon – on time, but no thanks to me – and as I was dropped off at the door the dread sank in. This was only the start of a very long day. The session itself was in a hidden studio, nestled away unassumingly on the top floor of a hotel. It wasn't long after I'd exchanged introductory pleasantries with my arranged writing partner that I had to excuse myself under the guise of using the bathroom. I had felt a singe of pain married with a tugging feeling – something was wrong. I locked myself away in one of the cubicles. I put the lid down, planted myself on the seat and took a deep breath as I assessed the damage. My arm had scabbed around my shirt, so when I stretched, I tore it off. In this moment I felt helpless. I had no plasters or bandages and I couldn't let the cut air-dry. I was going to have to make it through the entire session, another six hours, while bleeding. So I did. It was hell.

Since my mind was so consumed with the realities of the moment, I ended up writing about it. The song we wrote that day went on to become 'Rewritten', the debut single for Teske de Shepper, a Dutch YouTuber turned singer. I decided that I couldn't release it myself. It had to be a song for someone else. The lyrics came from a poem I'd written a few days before.

I can tell you have lived
by the marks on your skin
the lines carved on your face

from smiling so much
the hallow concave
under your eyes
from the many a late night
you've had the almost non-existent remains
of the acne you acquired from your teenage years
what may not be visible from a first glance
are the scars on your wrists that I have wished for many a night
could be shaken and removed like an etch a sketch
but these are marks of the wars you've fought some may say you've
*   lost*
but I believe each pale white bump and every purple tinted battle
*   scar is proof*
that you are indeed you.

'Rewritten'

I can tell you've lived by the marks on your skin
These are like the pages of a book
The lines beside your eyes let me know that you have smiled
A little more than I ever could
And I know that you can't sleep at night
For the hollow bumps beneath your eyes
Tell me more than stories ever could
You are not an etch-a-sketch
These marks engraved upon your flesh
Are indeed what make me love you

Under usual circumstances during these writing sessions, I'd have a track written and recorded in the same day, but I had to call it quits early on this one. For obvious reasons. I don't recall what happened on the journey home except ordering an Indian takeaway and an intense desire to go to bed. But all that pain – emotional and physical – wasn't enough to make me stop.

Between the Lines

I wasn't an everyday cutter. Just like I wasn't an everyday drinker. I would binge. I'd go weeks without thinking about it, but once I did, I hit it hard. It's a common misconception that self-harm is synonymous with suicide. I'd cut my arms, yes, but I never slit my wrists. Instead, I would daydream of my death often. I'd plan out every detail of the how, when and where. I've written more suicide notes than I have letters. One of the reasons why I never completed the transaction was due to my religious upbringing. I was taught that to knowingly take your own life was a mortal sin. According to my Catholicism, I was merely a steward for my own body; life and form are a gift from God and we were taught not to be negligent or destructive. So, I was trapped in a moral paradox: stay alive and continue harming myself in fear of the sin of suicide, when to do both is sinful. Instead, I wished for a consequential death, one where it looked accidental to others but was in fact a culmination of reckless endeavours. I stopped looking both ways when I crossed the street, hoping someone would hit me. I drank myself into oblivion, hoping to choke on my own vomit. I'd take sleeping pills and have a bath in the hope of falling into a slumber and slipping down into the water, never to emerge. I'd take the most dangerous route home late at night. I'd daydream that a bolt of lightning would strike me down. I lived that way for a long time, in a state of wanting to get help, wanting to feel better, but I was unwilling to actually change my behaviour.

It was around this time that quite a few people suggested I try cognitive behavioural therapy (CBT), a form of talk therapy aimed at teaching coping mechanisms. As it turned out, my mother knew just the man. I was promptly booked in for a session. I was hopeful that this could be the change I was looking for. The therapist was lovely, and he reassured me that everything we discussed would remain between us. He established that he knew who I was, but he didn't really watch "that sort of thing". When the session was in full swing, I rattled off my list of lengthy mental ailments, offering only enough information to ensure I was being honest but not showing him all my cards, just in case he would suggest a lobotomy, or something that would rob me of my chance to do music. I tiptoed around the topic of alcohol. I told him enough to know I was using it as a weapon of self-harm but not enough for it to be seen as a catalyst. My retelling of life events took up the majority of time we had booked together. The last ten minutes were focused on my current situation. When he asked me how I was, I had to stop and think for a while. I had no real answer for him. "Obviously, I mustn't be doing good as I've ended up here, but to tell you the truth, I don't know. I'm on an emotional delay usually." He shot me a look to suggest 'go on', so I continued. "I don't really know how I feel until after a day or so. Even then, are they my true feelings or my interpretations of how I should feel? Because I don't feel anything right now." This led to me explaining my overall feeling of numbness. Before I left, he told me something I've never forgotten. "Sometimes you've just got to watch videos of surfing dogs on the internet." And with that, I departed, and went straight to my friends' house and got drunk. Instead of sitting down in solitary confinement and facing the issues I addressed, I wanted to go be with my friends and get wasted. I never processed any of it.

On my returning session, a few weeks later, I was more suicidal than ever before. As I explained to him this time, "It's not like I've had some sort of traumatic life, I haven't. I'm just broken." I began to use chess as a metaphor. "Life is like a game of chess," I told him. "We all have our own personal chess board, trying to get to the end without losing too many pieces. In my own game of chess, I am merely a pawn, and every move I make loses another piece. The only wise move would be to eradicate me from play. With my elimination, all the other pieces would be free to continue their lives. No longer burdened by the pawn who can't play the game. They could live without worry of what I was going to do next. They could finally move on with their lives. No more guilt, fear or worry. It's the only logical solution…".

When I was done with this nihilistic rant, I looked to him. There were tears in his eyes that he quickly wiped away. He said: "Don't you think that they will find something else to worry over? Humans always will." We came to a moot point. I was unwilling to change, so what was the point in carrying on? This led to the conclusion from both of us that maybe CBT wasn't for me after all.

There were no hard feelings; he'd just admitted there was nothing he could do. That was my last CBT session. Ever.

Cover Story

I often forget that, to strangers, the scars on my arms are shocking and horrific. To me, they're just my arms. I always cover up most areas of my body that I am insecure about. For example, I don't like my lower stomach so I always wear high-waisted jeans. I dislike my biceps so I refrain from capped sleeves. As my forearms aren't something I get insecure about, it wasn't second nature to cover them up. A few times, this caused headaches for my management, who are now experts in defusing bombs when it comes to hiding my health issues. A few years ago, my team once stopped a red top newspaper from running a story about my self-harming, alongside printing pictures that proved it. I must've seemed remarkably fragile, for even the paper themselves, I would learn, were afraid that the publication of the story would lead to my suicide, and they didn't want to be held accountable for the death of a teenage girl.

But, how did they get the story?

In aide of promotion for my debut album, *Running with Scissors*, the paper was running a feature on me. Nothing more than a puff piece about the album, I was told. Instead, they ended up with a scoop that they could never have anticipated. In advance of the photo shoot for the piece, I'd answered all their innocuous questions. On the day of the shoot, all I had to do was turn up and smile. I had my hair, make-up and styling done for me by a professional. It was a rare occurrence at the time for me to agree to such a photo shoot; it'd been over a year since my last one, not since I was part of *The X Factor*, and I felt out of my depth. I was extraordinarily self-conscious. I was shy, withdrawn and struggled to express myself – the exact opposite of where I needed to be. I knew why. When it came to covering my scars, I couldn't. The stylist was even in the changing room with me, something I wouldn't normally allow. Due to the time restriction, I just had to go with it. No one mentioned my arms and I did my best to choose strategic poses. I left that day defeated. I didn't want to think of what the outcome would be. But they knew. Everyone in the room knew. It wasn't until a few days later when I got a phone call from Rick that I knew. The journalist had been in contact with my PR team and wanted to know if I'd be willing to approach the article from a different angle. If not, they were going to make up their own narrative and use the images to accompany it. I'd already signed my release form so they were within their rights to do so. I agreed to re-do the interview, it would've been foolish not to. The journalist was sympathetic and respectful. We discussed the scars but with the aim of creating a dialogue about mental health for others. It felt oddly freeing to do so – I could perhaps no longer live in shame and have to be all secret about it.

In the end, thankfully, the story never ran. But this wasn't the last time my scars were discussed in public circles. My team had to send out so many emails about the marks on my skin. This only lessened when I resorted to letting my arms heal. Once the wounds

closed up, I could cover them effectively. But, with the album out, and more and more journalists and press people wanting to speak with me about my music, it became clear that my arms were now a no-go zone. This, unfortunately, led to a new, much less conspicuous canvas for me to make my mark – my thigh.

Unlike with my arms, there was no gradual build-up of smaller wounds. For my thigh, I went straight in for the kill. One evening, in spring 2014, while staying at my manager's house, I decided to mix a potentially deadly concoction, consisting of a handful of sleeping pills and painkillers and several large glasses of hard liquor. I set out to hurt myself like I'd never done before. And, instead of a dinner knife, this time I opted for a different weapon: a large chef's knife. Before I took the blade in hand, I googled the most efficient way to sharpen it and spent some time ensuring the knife was as pointed as possible. I was going to do it properly this time.

After the first incision on my left thigh, I knew that I was in deep waters. The knife pierced the skin with an ease that I'd never experienced before. I started only cutting into the front part of my leg, making an incision from the inner thigh by my skirt line and cut upwards. "I'll still be able to wear summer clothes," I thought. It wasn't until I started nicking the outside of my thigh that I lost control. All the chemicals and medication kicked in at once. The endorphins from the cutting, the narcotics from the sleeping pills and the drowsiness from the alcohol overwhelmed me. When I came to moments later, I was scared. For the first time, I had gone too far. There were more than 30 wounds in my leg. Three in particular were causing me grave pain. I sat in a puddle of my own blood. The cuts wouldn't stop bleeding – one in particular was more than an inch wide. I needed help. The bleeding wasn't going to stop. I tried my best to clean myself up first. I grabbed paper towels and mopped down the floor. Though they absorbed the puddle, I was still bleeding heavily onto the floor tiles. I grabbed some disinfectant from under the sink, wiped the blade and put the knife in the dishwasher. With an increasingly foggy head I sat down and grabbed my phone. I sent a cryptic text to my manager, who was sleeping upstairs. I wrote: "I need help…" Within moments, I could hear a rustle from above.

I don't know what expression was on his face because I hung my head low. I couldn't face looking him in the eye. I had no words to express my fear. I don't remember the details but I remember sitting silently in the back seat of Rick's car, as he and his wife spoke as calmly as they could with each other. I was out of it.

We arrived at A&E around 2 a.m. I remember a very drunk man, sprawled out over three metal seats. There was a green bin liner with his things underneath him. As we approached the nurses' station the fear kicked in. I had to explain what I had done. I tried to mask my shame by saying one or two light jokes, none of which were found to be funny. Rick took over. I merely nodded when asked a question. After an hour of waiting, and more bleeding, I was taken into a cubicle. One of the first questions from the doctor's lips was, "Have you been drinking?" I explained that I'd had a glass of wine with dinner and also another drink when everyone went to bed. Though this was true, this wasn't a factual representation of the situation. I never mentioned that the drink was 90 per cent proof and that I'd taken pills too. The doctor quickly concluded that I required stitches. Somewhat ironically, I'm afraid of blood and needles. While I daydreamed, a commotion began brewing around my cubicle. As it turns out, word had got around the ward that I was there. Why anyone even cared is beyond me. This didn't stop a flock of nurses coming in and out of the room. They were coming in to have a look at what Janet Devlin had done to herself. To see it for themselves. Rick immediately became my bedside bouncer. As he recalls, he stood on the other side of the curtain with his arms folded, questioning the purpose of anyone who dared enter my room. It worked. But my night was far from over. With my leg in stitches, I was informed that I couldn't leave the hospital until two specialists from the hospital's mental health department had observed me. My eyes rolled at the thought of having to describe what I had done. It was time to play the sane game. Again. I was escorted to a plain white room, which I assumed was for grieving families. Though Rick and Cat came in with me, the two doctors politely asked them to leave. They sat down and began speaking in what I can only describe as the 'safe space' voice, a soft and comforting timbre employed by psychiatrists and counsellors. I switched on professional mode and adorned my best 'I know how this looks' smile. I knew what the doctors were looking for. They wanted a justification to keep me in for the night. On the inside, and perhaps because of the medication I took, I felt like a caged animal, trying to fight for my freedom. I stayed calm and answered every question as eloquently as I possibly could. When we established that I was indeed safe with Rick and Cat, and was in no way in danger there, they began asking the deeper questions. I explained how I knew that self-harm was a "redundant coping mechanism that only has short-term benefits, with lifelong consequences". I promised them I'd never do it again and that "the shame and guilt from the trip to A&E was the wake-up call I needed". They pushed the issue of sectioning me for "their peace of mind… and my own good". This was enough for me to beg: "Music is my life, you don't understand," I pleaded. "Music is what gets me out of bed in the morning in spite of the depression. When I've had suicidal thoughts, it's what keeps me from going over the edge. If you lock me up in here, you'll be taking away my only oxygen. Removing me from my schedule will only take away my purpose to live. Then this will become a suicide watch instead of a self-harm scenario…". For whatever reason, this worked. Reluctantly, very reluctantly, they let me go. In retrospect, I probably should've stayed, but on that particular night I wasn't ready to surrender. I wanted to do it on my own terms. I crawled into bed that morning with a heavy heart. I knew I had to change. I vowed to myself that I would never self-harm again. I downloaded an app called Days Since to mark the date. Again, I made a pinky promise with myself, and this time I meant it. I couldn't go through that again. This was the wake-up call that finally woke me up. Since April 11, 2014, I've been free from self-harm.

Life Lines

Sadly, the chapter doesn't quite end there. Though I no longer cut myself, I still bear the burden of my past on my body. You may have to look closely to see my scars, but they're there. In the wrong light, it's as if they glow in the dark. If I'm shooting a YouTube video or a music clip, I'm always careful when filming so as not to have my arm in shot, or at least as quickly and as little as possible. For the past five years, I have almost forgotten their presence. Every now and again they remind me that they're still there. When

I catch my reflection in the mirror, my eyes look to my arms first.

Today, I choose to use the scars as a positive affirmation, a symbol for the darkness I once lived through, but the proof that I survived. I once had a life I couldn't handle, an existence I yearned to be free from. These scars are a reminder that my darkest days are done. The shadow did not prevail. I am not disillusioned by the notion of others reacting the way they do. How is a stranger to know that I am not still fragile? To sane people, the very concept of cutting into themselves in order to feel *something* is beyond comprehension. For this I am glad. When my scars are met with ignorant remarks, I am happy. To know that someone else is stable and content enough to have never experienced this itch is a blessing. In this case, ignorance truly is bliss. I will not lie and say that these marks do not bring me shame. On the rare occasion I let my barriers down enough to touch them I recoil. If someone is to wrap their hand around my thigh I freeze. With every bump a friend's fingertip grazes, I sink a little further inside. No one ever mentions it but that doesn't stop my mind from racing over it. Do people think I'm weak? Do people think I'm mentally unstable? For a moment, it makes me feel worthless. For a moment I feel vulnerable. But only for a moment. Then the moment is gone. For I am no longer made of glass. I've let bygones be bygones. My past is my past. I do not live there anymore.

Cinema Screen

I've been laying wide awake watching every last
mistake I ever made. On a Cinema screen on the
back of my forehead.
I've been praying for a change hoping I could press
play on a different day. But we are the scene I
can never stop watching

And I've been trying to get everything you said
out of my head. I've been trying to move but all I
want to do is forget. And I'm dying to turn it off
I've been trying with all that I've got

And I know, you're no good for me
and I know, I know I should be
moving on, mooving on from this hollywood dream
on my cinema Screen.

I believed in all your lies. I've been crying through
the night. You never loved me. So why can I still
taste you between my teeth and I can feel you on
my bones and this pain just feels like home
lights camera action. I'm lying again

I've been thinking again, over thinking again
pushing me round the bend again.
tip- toeing over the edge. Trying my best to pretend
that I am not loosing myself.

Chapter Four

CINEMA SCREEN

I was 15 when I started my self-destructive disappearing act. At least, that's what I called it. You will know it by another name: anorexia. The catalyst for this behaviour I am still oblivious to. I've always possessed a level of discomfort within my own being, but I was foreign to this form of deleterious practice. Even at this age I understood that my perception of myself was undeniably warped. So, instead of obsessing over my reflection in the mirror, I put my faith in a set of weighing scales and worshipped the numbers as they began to decline.

My obsession with my weight did not arrive overnight. It was a gradual and slow descent into the grip of sheer insanity. By the end, I'd become a professional deceiver. I told lies on a daily basis regarding my food intake. I even lied to my doctor's face. He believed me. I was disappearing not only physically but mentally too. The only people I confided in were fellow sufferers, those who were also victims of the same affliction. I remember the denial. I remember believing every negative thought as if it were scripture. That I was "not thin enough", that I was "unlovable" and that I was "worthless".

Depression can come in a heartbeat or it can evolve and emerge over a period of weeks, months, or even years. I started realising that my 'black dog' began hanging out with me at the start of my teens, just as I was beginning to discover music and songwriting. The two arrived simultaneously. The darkness and the light to fight it. Music was everything to me... but, for many years, it wasn't enough to counter my internal battle against all manner of forms of self-sabotage. While my depression was to break through the surface in various disguises, not even in my bleakest nightmares could I have predicted that it would emerge through something I would need every day to survive: food.

Admitting you have a problem is the first, and biggest, step to conquering the problem. That day came for me during a PE class at school. I remember the moment as if it had happened this morning. I asked the teacher if it'd be OK for my best friend, Megan, and me to walk some laps of the pitch instead of participating in the lesson. I must have looked serious. Permission was granted, and we wandered far from the rest of the class.

"I have something to tell you," I told Megan, my voice weak, crackling with fear. She waited until I was ready to speak. Eventually I broke the silence and confessed everything to her. Words that I can only just bring myself to write.

"I have a serious problem," I said. "I don't know how to stop." I needed to tell her the rumours were true.

A mixture of disappointment and shock hung in the air but only for a second. I was met with a warm embrace and gratitude for my honesty, but I could feel the hurt in her arms. That's how I know the friendship we have is genuine. Today, she remains one of my best friends. For an hour I confided in her. I told her about all the lies, the pain and the suffering. I apologised profusely for my deceit and she accepted it.

"It's not the fact that you lied to me," Megan said. "I'm just sad that you couldn't tell me sooner. I would've tried to help."

These words broke me. I explained why that was the exact reason I didn't tell her. In the madness and the maelstrom, I didn't want saving. But now I did. I was finally ready to let her – anyone – help me.

Today, now, when I tell people I suffered with anorexia, they just imagine me as "15-year-old Janet", just a teenager who had no real understanding as to what the world was. In the intervening years, I'd been on primetime TV every week for three months, I'd been a success on *The X Factor*, I was in the public eye with my whole future ahead of me – how could I have problems?

To most people, it's assumed that the illness died before I even entered *The X Factor* at the age of 16. But that's far from the truth. Unlike any other addiction, with anorexia, you can't just say 'no'. It haunts me every day – not only my behaviour, but also my lack of concern for my own self. Eating food is a necessity. To want to live without it was to face a challenge that would come to almost destroy me. For years, I binged, purged and starved. I was anorexic. I was happy/miserable.

I have wanted to recount my struggle with anorexia in the hope that it would help others, especially those who are kind enough to follow my social media, afflicted with the same illness, to let them know that despite all the darkness that lay at the core of my being, a light always shone through, even when it felt there was none. To tell this story, not even the first chapter of terrible events during my formative years – a time defined by depression, body dysmorphia, illness, self-harm, alcohol abuse, and more, much more.

Friends and Foes

My self-destruction act really kicked into gear when I turned 15. The rapper B.o.B was all over the radio and TV with 'Airplanes', a song that to this day evokes memories of this period – just one song in a list of many that I have ruined by attaching them to moments of my own annihilation. Were you to sit beside me and ask where this behaviour came from, I would be able to mumble a few supposed reasons, but I can't quite pin it down. I've always possessed a level of discomfort within my own being – and I'm not alone in that, I know – but why on earth I turned food into the enemy is something that I hoped writing this book and exorcising some demons would shine a light on. What can I say, I'm a work in progress. And while I cannot pin down the root cause of my own lack of self-worth, I can pinpoint the object of my affection that started it all: the weighing scales that taunted me from the bathroom cupboard. They became my closest friend and, simultaneously, foe. I can visualise them in my mind, even now – the brand, what they looked like, how much they weighed when I picked them up and sneaked them into my bedroom. Even at such a vulnerable age, I understood that my perception of myself was undeniably warped.

I put my faith in these scales and worshipped the numbers as they began to decline. Just being able to write that sentence out loud today feels, ironically, as if a weight has been lifted from my shoulders. I would encourage anybody who feels the same to do so. I've been wanting to write this down for such a long time. My teenage diary was never enough.

In the beginning, it was the little things. I turned my nose up at all sugary treats and junk food. A few months later, things got increasingly worse. I moved out of my family home to go live with my grandmother, two miles away in the same village, but far enough. Away from my mother's constant worry and exhausting concern, I was free to indulge in my obsession. My weight plummeted to just six stone three pounds, but I wanted – needed – to go lower. Much lower. If people stared at me for too long, or asked why I was so thin, I would tell lies. I was disappearing not only physically but mentally too. I rarely spoke. I had discovered an innate ability to persistently say 'no' to myself. I'd acquired a vast array of tactics for how to hide my disordered behaviour, like stuffing chips down my gym socks when no one was looking, only to realise later they'd been so hot I'd actually burnt my ankles – that was a low point. Occasionally people would make comments on how I needed to eat more. It is from these days of exile and exclusion that my shyness derives today. The only reason I can go on TV and YouTube is because of my passion for performing my music – take that away and I feel like I have nothing to say. Instead of thinking about who was snogging who, all I remember thinking was "I'm not thin enough" and that I was worthless. In those lonely nights at my grandmother's house my disorder kept me company. It understood me. It understood my thinking. I was not going to let anyone take away the only thing I had. So, I continued hiding it until I could hide it no longer. In the midst of all the madness I'd occasionally write in my diary. One entry talked about my reasoning for not having ended it all yet. My justification for this was simple and stark. I did not want people to see my double chins as I lay in my coffin.

School's Out

My final year of secondary school is when my anorexia truly took a hellish form. My strictest regime of non-eating was allowed to flourish. I would refrain from eating anything for the five days of the school week. My diet consisted of Pepsi Max, peppermint chewing gum and black coffee. Light-headedness became the norm. Stomach rumbles were my body's applause for my willpower. I would only weigh myself once a week, every Saturday morning. I would crawl out of bed, exhausted but excited. Anticipating the decline. My mood lay in the balance of the result. In the beginning when the excess fell off, I was in euphoria – a happiness that now comes from completing a song. I was never exceptional at anything, so I came to crave the sense of accomplishment. It wasn't until weight loss had become harder that I began to feel the true torture. When the number wasn't what I wanted I'd be distraught. Inconsolable. The mixing pot of failure and being emotionally strung out from days of not eating was sheer hell.

At the weekends, I had to eat. I needed to maintain the facade of "I'm fine". There's something inexplicably intoxicating about eating for the first time after fasting for a few days. I was oddly in love with the feeling of it. I would easily consume over 2,000 calories in just one sitting alone. If it were there, I would eat it. Anything I could get my hands on. I couldn't keep it down though; this freedom of consumption only came from the knowledge I could purge later. So, I always would. Accompanied by music on full blast in the bathroom. Usually, Fall Out Boy or whatever heavy rock I had on CD.

School became ever more difficult. I was both mentally and physically exhausted. Sleeping became my safe haven. And music, too. I was listening to an ever-growing mix of influences. I was writing lyrics in my diary every day. I didn't think they were any good, but every now and again there was a line or a thought that I liked, and it was saved for when I would write a song, which was happening more and more often. As the confidence of losing weight came, so too did the joy of writing a song – as if I couldn't have one without the other. Of course, it didn't come without its difficulties. My waking hours had become all-consuming thoughts over something I wasn't even allowing myself to have.

Sleep was freedom from my thoughts, hunger and self-loathing. Alas, this would quickly become tainted too. Lying down became painful. No manner of nighttime positioning would result in comfort. Bruises were an everyday accessory that hurt at night. What was truly pathetic was the bedwetting. Whether it was a physiological or psychological reflex, I'm still unsure. Probably a combination of the two. I would drink endless bottles of water before bed to drown out the stomach cramps. I'd been a bedwetter as a child, so I knew exactly what to do when this occurred. You'd imagine consequences like this would be enough to make you step out and re-evaluate yourself. They're not. I continued to get progressively more ill. One night, I remember, I snuck out of bed at 2 a.m. and stepped into the late autumn night. My parents had quite a significant lane leading up to their house. It'd been recently tarmacked, so it felt like stepping onto the running track again. I proceeded to sprint up and down for as long as I physically could. The cool air and lack of stamina brought me to my knees. It left me throwing up violently into a drain at the side of the house. It wasn't until I tasted blood that I called it a night.

I'd created my own life ritual that I believed was beyond that of a 'normal' person. I saved up my generous £5 daily food allowance so that I could spend it on diet pills and black coffee.

Friends and peers had begun to express their concerns in different ways. The kids in my class would jest about me being so small I could fall down the cracks in the pavements or jokingly remark that I might blow out the window when they opened it. I received these as compliments. My friends began speaking about

me behind my back and asking questions they really didn't want the honest answers to. My uniform had started to make me look like a bag of bones in a boxy blazer. While my peers were sinking tequila, I was necking shots of vinegar. Instead of cotton candy, I was eating cotton wool. By this point it had become common practice for me to get the late bus to school. The sheer exhaustion of existing with an eating disorder meant that I would miss my first three classes at least once a week. Since my grades didn't suffer, at first, it was never really questioned. I would use the same excuse of a non-existent orthodontic appointment. Some days I would have to be picked up from school early. It was rare enough for me to blanket it under 'woman troubles'. I'd explained to anyone who dared ask that "My periods make me light headed" – which was excusable, as many do suffer that side effect. It couldn't have been more ironically far from the truth – my periods had stopped months before. I'd taken this as a more of a milestone than a red light. If anything, it was the green light to keep going.

There was a glimmer of hope beginning to shine through the self-inflicted darkness. I was starting to improve on my drumming. I decided that this was going to be the path for me. I was never one for the spotlight, but I'd always dreamt of being in a band like my heroes before me. I loved playing and it suited my personality. I could be at the very back of the stage but still be fundamental to holding everything together. I even chanced my arm in asking my mother if I could possibly have a drum kit for my birthday/ Christmas. After finding out the price of one, she promptly declined. This only made me more dedicated to getting one.

One day I saw a poster for a local singing competition. The prize money was substantial. First place walked away with £500, second place £200 and third place was £100. I figured that if I could at least place, I would be able to save up quicker to get my kit. I managed to get second place! This led to me competing in numerous local contests. My area was well and truly engulfed in *X Factor* fever, so these contests were frequent. Within three months I managed to save enough to get my Pearl Forum FZ kit! What I didn't anticipate at the time was actually doing quite well in the competitions. People began to know that I sang. My best friend even went as far as to buy me a video camera for posting singing videos. Which then lead to my mother sending one of my covers to *The X Factor* as my audition. "What's the worst that could happen Janet? They say no?" That "no" never came. I was thrust into the television spotlight and my life changed forever. The plus side was that my anorexia was completely at bay during this time. For when my mind was occupied with a to do list that was music related, I didn't feel the need to starve myself. I didn't want to starve myself. I wanted to be the best version of myself since millions of people were watching me. Luckily my demon went to sleep for a while, only to resurface a few years down the line.

The Why Factor

And keep going it did. For two years. Like many people suffering with an illness they can't, or don't, want to admit, I believed I had everything under control. I had my music. My songs. My voice. It was a distraction that kept everything underneath from growing to monstrous levels. I was working harder than ever before.

I was recording and releasing a single, starring in a movie, writing and recording two songs for the soundtrack, recording and releasing an EP to come out later in the year and also making a minimum of one video a week for my YouTube channel. Every single project had its own drop-down menu, each with a million things that needed to be done in order for everything to move smoothly. Contrary to what may be assumed, I was in fact happy. I love nothing more than to be busy. I was to film the music video for 'Outernet Song' days after the movie wrap. This kept me focused on set. My diet consisted of coffee, diet energy drinks and my one meal. I'd be up at 6 a.m. and in bed for midnight. This lasted less than a week, but I could see the results when filming had ended. People had begun to notice my weight loss. There was a cautionary compliment of "You look great but please don't lose any more weight!" I weighed in on the morning of the filming at 103 pounds. I was on the 'fine line' of looking good on camera but being waif in the flesh. We've all heard the expression "the camera adds 10 pounds", and this is sad but true to me. The people closest to me didn't seem to notice as quickly as everyone else. Acquaintances, friends, family is the order of people noticing change. Those who spend the most time with you are the last to be aware of it. The twisted thinking is always there. Every "You look too thin" or expression of concern was taken as a compliment. I didn't hear the pleas; I only heard the applause. It didn't take long for it to become serious. Meetings and phone calls about it were going on behind my back. When I was questioned, I continued to feign ignorance. I claimed that it was just stress related – buyable because I was working 17-hour days at times and I never truly had time off.

When I developed anorexia as a teen, I used to marvel at the control others had. How were they able to have a little bit of food and then stop? Somewhere along the way I picked up this ability too. There was no such thing as an 'ultimate goal weight' for me anymore. I didn't need one. I could see online, every day, that people were much smaller than me. There had been a lot of scandal around a particular female YouTuber at the time. It was clear that she had problems and it garnered the attention of many news headlines, media outlets and even my favourite YouTubers talking about it. If she could survive, keep a fan base and be so tiny, then so could I. People defended her against accusations of "promoting anorexia and unhealthy body image". That was my underlying fear throughout all of this. I never once wanted to be seen as a trigger warning. I didn't want anyone to look at me and say, "I want your figure". When they did, I'd pull them up on it. "It's not healthy to want to be this small! I don't want to be this size and I'm trying my best to get to a healthy weight." I used to lie like this to mask my guilt. I blocked out all thoughts of potentially being someone's 'thinspo'.

My internet followers would take my side. Defending me when someone left a hateful comment. They were under the belief that I was trying to fix it and that I was already insecure about it. I talked openly about despising the notion of being someone's inspiration.

I'd get emotional about it on camera because it was true. The hardest thing about anorexia is trying to explain the getting caught. On one hand, you want nothing more than for it to be your own secret. For no one to ever find out. In reality, you just want it to be socially acceptable. Just a thing that everyone knows about but for there to be no stigma and no consequences. Somehow you would be left alone to fade away without any judgement and be allowed to live your everyday life. These are obviously the delusions of a haunted person.

I was burning out. Somehow, I managed not to get ill that year. As everyone around me was catching colds, I remained unscathed. Yet another rebuttal to arguments of my ill health. I was embarking on my third UK headline tour. It kicked off at the end of November and carried on right through to Christmas. I was excited but for all the wrong reasons: I was going to be completely unsupervised for longer periods of time. Being the only girl on tour, I was able to have a hotel room all to myself. On the road, I didn't have a binge day, I would just eat whatever I wanted for one meal. I would also allow myself to have breakfast from time to time. This would either be a mocha or a croissant but never both. This led to everyone being even more perplexed as to how I was able to remain so small. I even overheard them defending me to audience members. Any concerns for how gaunt I looked were met with a "We know but we see her eat all the time!" As the tour continued the more bewildered everyone became. How was it that I was still managing to lose weight? They were unaware of my one true commandment. That I was in no way allowed to eat when I was on my own. This meant that I would usually fast for 18 hours a day. This was manageable as we'd have breakfast so late. I remember one time willing my body just to grab the Cheerios that were always around, but to no avail. I would've cried if I weren't so petrified. I shook it off and agreed with myself that I would try again later. I went back to that same spot six, maybe seven times and still nothing. I couldn't. I wasn't allowed to. The voice inside my head was patronising me with "It's not four o'clock yet! It's not four o'clock yet! It's not four o'clock yet! It's not four o'clock yet! It's not four o'clock yet!" It was also known by everyone that I would never eat three hours before a show. This left a very clear window in my day for when I would eat. Concerns only grew, from everyone. I just didn't understand what the big deal was. "So what, I'm skinny! Can we leave me alone now?" was a looping thought. I couldn't understand why the new 'body positivity' movement wasn't protecting me. The saddest thing was that throughout all this I really believed I was in control. That I could stop whenever I wanted to, I just didn't know when. I said that as soon as it became 'too much' I'd just start eating again. I believed the same lie I told myself about alcohol, that once it started interfering with my work I'd stop. This allowed me to keep going. I was working, and I was working hard.

The Moment of Truth

The last two shows of the My Opium tour were in Northern Ireland. These are always the most stressful of all. I have to become

the tour manager as well as the artist. Budgets were tight so we couldn't afford to fly my manager over to help orchestrate it all. There was no money for hotels, so the band stayed at my parents' home with me. I arrived the day before the boys did. When my mother greeted me at the airport, she couldn't hide her horror. When she attempted to steer the conversation that way I would abruptly interject. I'd told her that I wanted to see the local doctor over the holidays, that I knew something was wrong but there was nothing I could do until I had seen him. In the following days, she persisted in making jabs. Even in front of the band and asking their opinion. I greeted them with an eye-roll and a look of "are we really going to start this?" I always made sure she'd seen me eat; I needed her to believe my lie too. None of my family members said anything to my face. Even my oldest brother, who is famous for his brutal honesty, said nothing.

When the tour was over, so began the holiday season, the most dreaded time of the year for anyone with an eating disorder. My biggest issue with being at home initially was the fact I didn't have any scales there – well, we did, but they magically didn't work. The anxiety of not knowing how much I weighed was eating me alive. It made me even more controlling.

On December 19 I managed to buy some. It was my deceitful nature at its worst. I was going to get my hands on some scales, so help me God. Both my mother and I went off to do some Christmas shopping. I needed to pick up presents and she needed to pick up food. Perfect, we wouldn't be shopping together. I needed something to put the scales into. Sorted, I always carry around a shoulder bag large enough to hold more than that.

When we arrived at the shopping park, we parted ways. First port of call was Argos. I'd already ordered and paid for the scales online, so all I had to do was pick them up. Once I did that, I headed to the farthest shop from where my mother was. It was a ladies clothing store. I needed something to cover the scales in my bag. I opted for a dressing gown, as it appeared the most sizeable and inconspicuous. When the lady at the counter asked me if I needed a bag, I smiled and said "Yes, but only for the pyjamas." I gestured to my shoulder "I can fit the dressing gown in here". I could've easily fitted both, but I needed the bag. I had to have something to show my mother that I had been shopping when she asked what I got.

When I made it home that night, I was ecstatic. I had pulled it off – for now. I had to ensure that no one could find them. Where wouldn't my family look? We don't have locks in our house, so I knew when I left that room, they'd have a free for all searching. I opted for under the mattress. No one looked there but I could tell they looked everywhere else; I knew they'd been looking because I'd leave things in very specific places. For example, I'd leave a red sock in the top drawer, in the right hand corner and half folded over. When I came back, it was still there but it had been moved. I was being watched and I knew it. On December 21 I weighed in at my lowest weight of 96.7 pounds. I can't explain how proud I was of myself. After the weigh in I took a photograph of myself in my new avocado pyjamas. I had no intentions of ever posting it anywhere.

When I woke up on Christmas Day, I decided I would post the photo on my social media. The intent was innocent. I cracked a joke about how I'd hated avocados for years but I'd since learned to love them. I uploaded the photo and got stuck into the festivities. Little did I know, a storm of concerned comments were flooding in. Thick and fast. When I pulled up my accounts, I was in shock. This was a photo too far for strangers, fans and friends. The hate was immeasurable. This photo managed to turn even my most caring fans against me. There was no point in deleting it, that's a rookie mistake. Once something's been uploaded to the internet, it can never be taken down. I decided to delete comments. Any comment that addressed the weight and not the pyjamas was deleted. Which then led to me having to tell the commenters what I was doing, to stop them from speculating over it. I could sense that even the malicious comments were coming from a caring place. No one wanted to see me like that. Even I didn't. I couldn't look at myself without despising my reflection. This was the first time I had been faced with the real truth. It hit me. Like a ton of bricks collapsing on my chest I realised that I had no control anymore. My mind flashed back to when I first admitted to Megan I had a problem. I was back on that school playing field all over again. Why didn't I do anything then? How could I let things get worse? I felt worthless. But, I had also hit the hardest of rock bottoms. Finally.

Afterword: Recovery Position

So, when was my miracle? When did the demons disappear? What was my catalyst for recovery? To say I had one would be a lie. I have starved, purged and binged since the 'avocado' post. Following that moment, I went vegan. I figured that if I was going to be so intent on having food rules, I may at least make them beneficial. I fully understand that this is an issue unresolved. I am aware that it could be dangerous, but it saved my life in a way. I was able to get excited about food again. I allowed myself to eat freely again. The voice in my head that craved regime and regulations was pacified with a new set of 'dos' and 'don'ts'. It was a slow process but gradually the voice grew quieter and quieter, until one day I realised I didn't look for the calorie count on everything I bought. The mental calculator has been silenced. It took months for me to stop weighing myself. It took a year for me to be OK with my own company, to be single, to look after myself. I learnt how to run, to cook and to practice self-care. I moved to London. I left the scales behind. I even let myself buy baggy jeans and other articles of 'banned' clothing. Yes, my recovery is flawed. Yes, I've come back to that familiar emptiness a few times. It seems only probable that I would. I am only human. I may have won the battle, but I haven't won the war. But, so long as there's a pulse in my veins and some food in my stomach, I have triumphed.

Speak

Oh Danny boy I thought that we were friends
oh Danny boy you're drinking again
And I'm wearing the red dress but I'm not asleep
and I never said yes do you know what that means?
oh danny boy, I'm living here in silence
'Cause it's our little secret, it's our little secret
it's our little secret, under the sheet
I shouldn't keep. I'm not ready to speak

Oh Danny boy the meadows are in bloom
Oh Danny boy oh how I trusted you
Now there's blood on the roses, a broken bouquet
the flowers are dying, they shrivel in shame.
Oh Danny boy, I couldn't tell the truth

'Cause it's our little secret, it's our little secret
it's our little secret under the sheet.
I shouldn't keep

But you can't see the bruises and I'm the one who loses
I cannot speak your name. But I started writing these
words that I've been fighting. So no one has to say.
That it's our little secret, it's our little secret.
it's our little secret. Under the sheet, I will not keep.
'Cause I'm ready to speak.

Chapter Five

SPEAK

It is wisely advised that one should never venture too far down the lanes of their own memory. At least, without adult supervision. I've never been one to heed the stark warnings of others and instead opt to learn from my own mistakes. If my life were a book, every pearl of wisdom would be a moment of foreshadowing. To this day, one of the earliest cautions I recall was my mother informing me of the danger of strangers. Little did I know that I would come a little too close to the power men wield without fear of consequence.

I still remember the first time my mother had to explain what rape was. I was four years old. It was a glorious day, where the sun didn't have to battle the clouds for the spotlight. My mother, grandmother and I were in the car, on our way back from a day out. The radio was turned up loud and the windows were wound down low. We listened to the five o'clock news. With a sorrowful tone the broadcaster announced the tragic tale of a young girl who had been kidnapped and raped. "What sort of monster would do such a thing? Imagine how that little girl must feel," said my mother. My granny let out a sigh, as if no words could express her thoughts more appropriately. In the backseat of the car, I piped up with a perplexing question: "What is rape?" I made eye contact with my Mum in the rear-view mirror but she quickly looked away. After a moment of reflection, she answered. "Rape is when someone touches your private parts without your permission." I nodded as if I understood but turned my attention to the fields out of my window. I mulled over what she had said for quite some time after that. I couldn't quite grasp the idea of why anyone would want to touch someone's privates, let alone my own. At school I'd been warned about kidnapping and why I should never take sweets from strangers. But other people touching my privates – why on earth would they ever want to do that?

A year later, I distinctly recall my mother – perhaps haunted by the radio broadcast the year before – had to ask me a difficult question. I'd come to her late one evening complaining of an itch in my "private parts". My mother grabbed her pot of Sudocrem from the cupboard and led me upstairs to her bedroom. She immediately removed my pyjamas and began to look at my genitals. She had jumped into a state of desperate action. She asked: "Has someone been touching you?" I was shocked and within a heartbeat I replied, "No, I swear, I swear no one has! I'd never let someone touch me!" Her voice calmed. She looked deep into my eyes – she knew when I was lying. And she always could tell when I was telling the truth. Still can. As she brought me close to her chest to comfort me, she told me that if anyone ever were to touch me that I must tell her immediately.

It was around six months later that something out of the ordinary happened. I have altered the names and details of the story – but, let me assure you, it did happen.

I was at a large house with my mother and brothers, along with some children from other families, some of whom were older. This age difference meant all the children could go and explore without an adult. That day we were all out revelling in the adrenaline of play. We decided we'd all venture up the hill and play among the hay bales. It was the perfect place for hide-and-seek and, as there were seven of us playing, it was going to be a long game. We decided that a boy a few years older than me would be the seeker. We knew there wouldn't be much time to play due to the raincloud lingering overhead. The countdown began. We all ran into the forest of plastic-wrapped silage. I could feel my little heart pounding in my chest as I ran. I decided it best for me to take the ground instead of on top of the bails – I didn't want to fall like I'd done before. Finally, I settled on a spot. I sat down and brought myself into the smallest ball I could make. I stayed there, silent, for what seemed like an eternity. I could hear one or two other children getting eliminated but they all seemed very far away. I thought I was safe but with a thud, the boy who was seeking jumped down from the bail, discovering my hiding spot. Before I had a moment to shout out that I'd been found, he put his finger over his lips and shook his head. "Don't worry, I won't tell them I caught you," he said as he sat down beside me. Just as I was about to get up, he reached for my hand and whispered, "I have a secret. Can you keep a secret, Janet?" I nodded enthusiastically. "I can and I'm really good at it too!" I responded innocently.

"Good," he said, "but put your right hand up to God and swear to him you won't tell." I obliged, raised my hand and swore to God and over my Mum's life that I wouldn't tell.

"Have you ever heard of snogging," he said. I shook my head.

"I'll teach you. Because you'll have to learn for when you're a grown-up." With that, he held my shoulders down and proceeded to French kiss me. I tried pulling away, but I was trapped. When I resisted, he just pushed closer and closer, until my head was against the bail. It wasn't until I tried to scream that he stopped. As he pulled away, he put his hand over my mouth and said sternly, "It's not that big of a deal! I'm just showing you now, so you don't have to learn later. I'm doing you a favour!" With his hand still over my mouth he reminded me of my promise and shushed me one last time. With that, he lifted me atop the bail and announced that I'd been caught. I hastily made my way back to the bike and joined the others, not saying a word of what happened.

When we made it home that evening, my mother could sense something was off. I tried explaining, as best I could, that I'd been told a secret and I couldn't tell her because she'd die. "I couldn't tell you anyways because I'd have to show you," I said. After pleading, I finally attempted to show my mother what I'd learnt. To her horror she obviously stopped me when she realised what I was doing. After again reassuring me that she would not die, I told her who taught me. In anger she stood firm and left the room. After that, I've no idea what happened. We never spoke of it again. One thing I know for certain is that my relationship with that boy was never the same again. To this day, I still freeze up when I hear his name.

First Kiss

I've always been one to take everything literally. If someone in authority tells me to do something, I will. The Church was my beacon of power. I grew up in a disciplined Catholic home, attended the local parish primary school and even became an alter server by the age of seven. I wanted so much to be good in the eyes of the Lord. Like a sponge I took every word of scripture and religious teachings to heart. I remember noticing that not everyone felt the same. There were those who were able to approach the Church with a more flexible adherence to the teachings. Though their lack of faith made me uncomfortable, it never altered my own integral belief system. I believed everything the Church teachings told me, right down to not looking at my own naked body. One Sunday, I remember being told that we must avoid lust for one's own body. So, I did my upmost not to. And, as you have come to learn, I have never thought much about my own body.

Luckily, I was not one to have crushes in school. I took this as a blessing as it would be one less thing I'd have to say in my confessions with my priest at church on Sundays. The more I learnt about sex, the happier I became to ignore feelings of lust. These feelings of ambivalence towards the opposite sex carried well into adolescence. By the age of 12, as my peers were attending local discos and contemplating snogs with strangers, I rejected every thought. As a result, I was teased for my absence and lack of desire to be desired. When friends would chastise me over it, I would lie: "I have kissed a boy before, you just don't know him!"

I confided in my best friend at the time and told her most of the truth. Instead of being supportive in my choices, she insisted that she'd "fix" it. After listing the boys in our year, she made me pick one. With this, she was to become matchmaker. "You've just got to get it over and done with!" I agreed. If it were known by my classmates that I'd officially kissed a boy, the teasing would end.

For the sake of the story, let's call the first boy to ever kiss me 'Bob'. Bob was an inbetweener who managed to be a part of every friendship circle at school. It was rare that someone could weave within groups; most of us pick a clique and stick with it. But Bob was naturally charming. He was a great songwriter and guitar player and was easily the closest thing I had to a crush at the time, hence why I chose him over the other boys. He took a lot of persuading to kiss me, from both my friend and me. He was adamant that he could not be my first kiss. I convinced him, on numerous occasions, that he wasn't. Finally, he reluctantly agreed. We were to kiss.

My friend arranged the whole thing. During break time, this friend told me to meet Bob behind the school, where the oil tank was. School children weren't allowed to go there, so we knew no one would be there. Naturally, I turned up early. I was so nervous. My hands were shaking and sweating profusely. I waited. Taking deep breaths. After a few minutes, I heard footsteps slowing approaching and I prayed to God it wasn't a teacher. It was Bob. As he emerged around the corner, he flicked his long fringe to announce his arrival. In that moment I wondered why he didn't just cut it enough to be out of his eyes. Surely his neck must hurt by the end of the day after the constant flicking?

Anyway, there were no signs of nerves in his demeanour and he approached me with a cocky yet sly grin on his face. I just wanted it to be over and done with. I accidentally let out a deep breath as he grabbed my hands. With one more flick of his hair, he pulled me in and we kissed. It was far from natural to me. I tried my best to enjoy it but the worry of whether or not I was doing it right overtook me. I'll be honest, it was a sloppy saliva-infused nightmare. Even though I had nothing to compare it to, I knew it wasn't good.

"What are you kids doing out here?" a man yelled.

As we pulled away, a string of spit kept us connected. I wiped my mouth and we ran back to the schoolyard. We parted ways at the canteen. As I hurried down the steps towards class, I locked eyes with my friend who was waiting. She began clapping giddily and asked me all of the questions under the sun.

"It was fine," I shrugged.

"I'm in his class now so I'll just ask him then!" she said, disappointed by my lack of salacious news.

As I made my way to class, school suddenly felt like a school out of a teen movie. Older kids were looking at me, whispering, laughing and pointing as they passed. My whole face began to blush bright red, a trait my mother blessed me with. I sprinted to the IT department where my next class was. It was a triple period lesson so I was going to be there for some time. I put my headphones in, started up Microsoft Word and made my way through our worksheet study notes. Even though phones were banned in school, people were using them as MP3 players, so they were allowed on the tables. One person forgot to put their phone on silent and as they were being yelled at, I pulled one ear out and turned around. As I scanned the room, I noticed a few people staring at me. Without hesitation, I raised my hand and asked for permission to use the bathroom.

"You should've gone at lunch!" the teacher scowled. I pleaded and was granted permission. "Never again," she said as she handed me the bathroom slip. The computer room was the farthest from all of the bathrooms, so I belted it through the corridors. "No running in the halls!" I heard a man's voice yelling from the maths room. I turned to face him, and my heart sank. The classroom had turned around to see who it was. In that moment I made eye contact with Bob. The class erupted when they saw me. They were howling with laughter. My eyes began to water as he mouthed, "I'm sorry". Before I could even apologise to the teacher he gestured for me to move on and told them to settle down. I was mortified. I couldn't run so I had to listen to the mean things they were saying. I hung my head in shame.

It was that bad of a kiss that everyone knew about it. Bob had told everyone. It was a very small school – news travelled fast. I locked myself in the bathroom stall and quietly cried myself into panic. It was too late in the day to call sick, so I had to just wait it out. The rest of the day was just as horrible as you can imagine. I earned the nickname 'Slobber' and took the rest of the week off. Just like most things, the heat had died down by the time I arrived back on Monday. I was still scarred. I stopped talking to almost everyone and shut myself off for the remainder of the year, and it wasn't until several years later that I found myself a small, but solid, group of friends.

Under the Covers

One summer, when I was 15, I went along with one friend to a party hosted by someone she knew and I didn't. When we got there, the party was in full swing, and everyone there was drinking, dancing and laughing. I was trying my utmost to be responsible, glugging a glass of water after every drink and sticking only to the alcohol I'd brought with me.

After a while, I was ready to go home but my friend wanted to stay a little longer, so I said I'd go and lie down upstairs until she was ready to leave together. As I was trying to get to sleep, a boy from the party came in the room and got into the bed next to me, claiming to be tired too. Though I was uncomfortable with the situation, I didn't want to make a fuss. I was drunk and tired. I tried to get to sleep and assumed he had too. Out of nowhere I could feel his hand slide up my dress and his palm come to rest on my upper thigh. I assumed that he'd move it as soon as he moved position again, and that it was just a sleep reflex. It wasn't. It was a test to see if I was sleeping. As I didn't move when he did this, he proceeded to move his hand inside my knickers. I froze. As his fingers continued to wander I snapped out of it and mustered up the courage to say "No!" in a firm whisper. I grabbed his hand and shoved it away. I made sure that he knew I didn't want that. Not that he'd bothered to ask anyway. With a monosyllabic mumble, he shuffled and went still again. I lay there, in complete shock of what had just happened.

A short while later, the silence was broken again by the same stirring. This time there was no test or warning. His fingers went straight to the inside of my underwear again. I froze for the second time and he got even further than he had done before. It was as if I'd mustered up all my courage in my initial outburst. I willed for my body to move but it wouldn't. It felt as though my every limb was weighed down by concrete. "Why is he doing this?", "Why won't he stop?" and "Why won't you fucking move, Janet?" were the questions screaming inside my head. After a few minutes – and it was minutes – I got so mad at myself that I managed to grab his hand again and remove it from inside me. I could feel his body tense with shock, as though he was surprised I was awake. "I said no!" I whispered loudly as I shoved myself off the bed and left the room. I went straight to the bathroom and slid down against the closed door. There I sat, on the warm tiles, staring at my feet. Battling to string a coherent thought together through the remaining daze of booze. Wishing with all my might that boy hadn't done what he just did. Wishing that I couldn't feel the ghost of his fingertips on my skin. I was left with more questions than answers. Mainly, what would he have done if I were asleep? With these thoughts filling my mind, I left the party without telling anyone what had happened.

I did finally tell my best friend a few days later. She was as shocked as I was. I told my counsellor too. When they asked what I wanted to do about the situation, I had no answer. I didn't know. I didn't want to cause a fuss over something that had happened while this boy was drunk. Though I must admit, it stung me to my core to think that there was no acknowledgement of what he had done. That was my own fault. I allowed that to happen by not wanting to make that moment all about me. To this day, I still think about what I should have said to him – just so he knew that what he did was not right.

I know this is by no means the worst sexual assault story. It happens to teenagers all over the world every day. Indeed, you can't open a newspaper today without reading much more terrifying events. But still, the actions of that one boy that night made a huge impact on me.

Heart-shaped Box

I keep the memory of what happened that night wrapped up tight in a box far, far away in the back of my mind. It's not something

that comes up in my everyday life, so I rarely have to think about it. I'm over it now.

But, despite that, it's left me with a lot of trust issues. When someone does something like that to you, it's hard to get back on the horse and trust again. It hasn't stopped me trying though. I do date a lot.

Today, I identify as a demi-sexual-bisexual, though I'm not one for labels. This sounds a little sesquipedalian and incredibly more complex than it actually is. To make things simple, let's tackle them separately. A demi-sexual is someone who only feels sexual attraction to someone after a strong emotional connection has been established. Basically, sex is the last thing on my mind most of the time. When I see someone attractive, my mind never wanders there. Instead, I have a silent applause for their magnificent gene pool. This also means that I've never had a one-night stand. Not because I don't want to or that I have anything against anyone who does, but because my mind simply isn't motivated enough to make it happen. Again, I have to trust and have an emotional connection with someone before I even consider the possibility. And that takes time. Anyone who calls me a puritan and a prude hasn't been paying attention. I am constantly reminded by people "what I am missing out on" but, in my mind, I really am not.

As for bisexual, that's understood. Some days I feel more pansexual than anything, giving no regard to the gender of the person I am dating. I've also been bashed – publicly in the press and privately – for the fact that I tend to date people much older than myself. Like gender, age has never come into the equation for me either. Like I often say, when God made me, he either used up a lot of spare parts and just threw me together, or he was aiming for something truly specific!

Honest men

Where have all the honest men gone? I'm flocked by
vultures in the summer sun. They take what they can
get, then gone in another breath. Where have all the honest
men gone?

My shoes are filled with lead what can I do. I'd
sink or swim or just avoid the truth.
So I'll take what I can get and accept the consequence
but where have all the honest men gone?

Cause there'll be tears in my eyes oh no surprise
Cause there'll be tears in my eyes till the day I die

So angel of death why haven't you kissed me yet
Oh angel of death I long for your caress
So won't you save me, oh save me
oh won't you save me, oh save me

Where has all my happiness gone? It disappeared the
moment I sang your song. I'll be buried in this
noose, it's written in the books. But where have all
the honest men gone?

My soul wasn't enough, you want it all, you wanted blood
But where have all the honest men gone?

Chapter Six

HONEST MEN

I was 16 when I met 'Voldemort', a man who was to have such an impact on my life it altered the path of my career forever. But, as I have learnt the hard way, for all the dishonest, devious and dark men who control the world, their direct opposites will always rise to cancel them out. At least, this was my experience.

Up until my appearance on *The X Factor*, when it came to my music, as a 'career', I had simply been singing my songs at local gigs and competitions and posting videos on YouTube. I had no idea how to get into the industry. After I invited *The X Factor* into my life, and following my success on and exit from the show, it wasn't long before a host of industry faces wanted to take meetings with me and recount tales of their success and glory of which I, too, could be a part. When my time on the show ended,

I was – like most of the contestants from the show – assigned a management company to oversee this crucial transition, from my normal life as a struggling/emerging artist into a 'breakout star', fresh and flushed from the visibility given to me by a national TV show whose audience was in the millions. I was offered deals from left to right; album deals, artist-led routes, offers from labels who weren't interested in doing it my way; even an offer from a *Dragon's Den* entrepreneur who wanted me to release singles I'd already sung on the show. I felt like a sponge, over-saturated with information that I couldn't process, totally wrung out and empty, full of holes.

In the midst of all this, I met various figures from across all corners of the music business. These people offered me words of advice and calming affirmations, and complimented me on my singing. It was so rare that I actually believed anything anyone said in those days, but their words were delivered so genuinely, so confidently, it was hard not to believe them. Even if I still could not believe myself. But I knew one thing to be true: I didn't just want to be sucked in and spat out of the show's machine. For better or worse, I wanted to do things on my own. When the time came and I left the show's assigned management company, I was trying to go it alone but not having much success in a world that was becoming increasingly hard to navigate as a solo female indie artist, fresh from a reality TV contest.

When I felt like I'd exhausted all options, and I'd slipped out of the attention of all the industry figures that had once offered me the world, out of nowhere, I was given an opportunity I could not pass up. This person convinced me that my dream of becoming a serious artist was about to come true. I reached out to 'Voldemort', someone to whom I was introduced during my time on the show, and was given all the signs that I was going to be broken as an emerging artist. He professed to having a lot of investment money so it would be financially beneficial for me too. Since I'd ploughed almost all my savings into my own development since leaving the show, it was exciting to think that professionals would now take me over the finishing line. Voldemort sent me to studios with songwriters with the aim of completing an album, and I spent every penny I had in the hope that I was making the right decisions and would receive advances and payments for my investment.

The outcome was far from what I expected. I became embroiled as a victim in a huge fraudulent label scam, which I'm unable to expand upon due to legal reasons. Services were engaged and my money was being spent on things of which I had no knowledge. I went into shock. It didn't take long for the feelings of depersonalisation to take over. And it numbed me to my very core. Every waking moment felt surreal. All of my demons came back to haunt me. My body was no longer my own; I had turned it over to my head. I felt as though I was living in a fantasy, completely separate from my own reality. My life had become the plot of the film *Catch Me If You Can*, when the character shapeshifts their way through the story, leaving disappointment and damage in their wake. There were so many questions. These people, these frauds, had robbed me of everything – my money, my dreams, my confidence, my ability to believe in myself. All the showmanship and talk of "You'll be a star, kid!" was just empty, hollow, meaningless words. Naturally, I beat myself up for falling for it. "How could I be so naive?"

I had been burned badly. On top of everything else my body and brain were fighting, I now had this to navigate. I became reluctant to make any inroads in righting myself on a path to music making. When I did reach out to labels I found they were overwhelmed and inundated with reality TV and talent show artists, so I just wasn't able to make any impact (as an "Axe-Factor" reject) in an oversaturated market. I had become just another victim of the show's success.

While all this chaos was unfolding, it was suggested that I try a crowdfunding campaign to help get my debut album recorded. I had the songs. Crowdfunding was a new concept at the time and wasn't as commonplace as it is now. I even had an interview with CNN about this 'new concept' making waves in the industry and whether it would become the future of music making. I remember people throwing scorn on the idea, but I had no other option open to me – it was the future I had to grab with both hands.

Because of the fans I'd gained during the show, the campaign started off really well, allowing me to start the recording process only a few months later. I began working on the album in Sheffield with a production team I met while on *The X Factor*, and a small start-up label came on board to help me release. I'd never made my own album before, so it was a whole new world. I had just enough drive to keep me going, even though I knew I was broken. When the album was almost complete, that's when it all fell apart. I just couldn't connect with what I had written. The music, the

words, the metaphors – even down to the production – they just weren't *me*. The trauma of the past year had affected my emotional state and I wasn't able to listen to the music. The feeling sat like a rock in my stomach. I would sit in the control room of the studio and listen to the tracks on the speakers. All I could hear were the reservations I had about the music.

At the same time as the album was awkwardly being pieced together, I was introduced to a new management team called Insomnia, run by Rick Chambers and Adam Low. My saviours, to this day, though I could never have known that at the time. I had wanted to work with them after the first time we met. Rick and Adam seemed cool and knew what they were talking about. I felt I could trust them. I had been looking for management for many months, so was delighted when Insomnia agreed to manage me. I started to feel positive again for the first time in a long time.

Then, just as quickly, things came crashing down around me once more. Rick and Adam began unearthing service agreements in my name, receiving angry phone calls and a barrage of emails from companies who said I owed them money – the scam in which I had been unwittingly involved had meant that I was now scores of thousands of pounds in debt. The full list of what I allegedly owed was finally laid bare and made for horrific reading.

It was Rick's unenviable job to call me one night to tell me I was now officially bankrupt. However, I had committed to a 14-date UK and Ireland tour as part of the crowdfunding campaign, which people had paid for and were expecting, so I had to dig deep in order to find a way to deliver, or risk losing the one thing that kept me going: my fans. Rick and Adam began paying me a weekly recoupable wage, and their support meant that I could work, eat and take to the road. It was a terrific – if terrifying – experience. I was touring music I didn't quite love, using money that I hadn't earned, but I learnt so much about what it meant to be a touring artist: much more than I ever learnt from the *X Factor* tour. From how to interact with an audience to how to manage stage fright on a day-to-day basis, this tour taught me what it was to be a working musician. I loved every minute of being on the road and it reaffirmed my choice to pursue music full time. It put me back on track.

Once the tour was over, I began trying to salvage what was left of my debut album. I had a release plan set with my previous label, but after continued differences around the overall vision, relations with the label broke down, as I couldn't bring myself to release something I wasn't proud of. We were rapidly running out of time, so after countless meetings Rick and I had an idea: we were going to re-record the whole album with a minuscule budget, aim for release, and do it all within six weeks. All we needed to do was find a producer, a studio and money to do it. We binned half of the songs on the original album and replaced them with songs I'd written more recently. In truth, I never really liked the album as it was recorded the first time round, as *Hide & Seek*. I simply didn't feel like many of the songs or the production represented who I really was. But, because of the whirlwind of *The X Factor* and my ongoing inner battles, I'm not sure I knew at the time who I was. Now you know why the record is called *Running with Scissors*.

Trying to pull off what we were trying to pull off was risky and dangerous, and we were warned against it. Before we even arrived at this idea, I'd already had my mind made up on ditching the whole 'Janet Devlin' project. I was going to rename myself as 'Juniper Daze' and reinvent myself. I even filmed a whole meeting I had with my team about it. Obviously it didn't happen in the end, and I braved the Janet Devlin hurricane. So, why so little time? I'd originally set a release date through the crowdfunding campaign and I'd already postponed it once, so I couldn't risk doing it again. Fans who had so lovingly pledged money were now growing increasingly frustrated by how long it was taking. We had no money to hire producers or musicians – all of the money raised had already been spent on recording the album in its first iteration as *Hide & Seek*. But in a short amount of time, Rick managed to find two producers who could work together in tandem on the album. They both had studios with a recording booth and access to lots of gear. One was very pop orientated and contemporary, the other very musically sensitive and old school. Neither had ever worked with another producer in this capacity before and though reluctant in the beginning, they really made it work. The money they received was modest but that didn't stop them putting love into the record. Not to mention the man hours.

As this chaos swirled around me, I was actively self-destructing too, abusing alcohol and self-harming. Rick became my guardian and minder, because I was incapable of doing many things myself. While all of this was going on, my fans were none the wiser as my team at Insomnia kept my social media presence active, and became pretty good at tweeting as a teenage girl!

Homeless and penniless, I quietly moved into Rick's home. I was living on a budget of £25 a week with Rick going into a debt hole to help me out of mine. I had nothing... and I was making other people's lives worse because of it.

Even after the completed album was released in July 2014, it took years to clean up the mess that was made. I can't take credit for an ounce of the clean-up either. If it weren't for Rick and all at Insomnia, the album never would've happened and my career would have almost certainly ended. Insomnia took on my debt, risking their own business by using up their cash flow in the

process. In the years since that it took to make up for those losses, I wasn't much help either. I was constantly almost on the brink of death through excessive alcohol consumption and struggling to keep it together. It's thanks to my team, I'm alive today. They stood by me while I rediscovered my love for music and my reason for living. For every session, release and gig they put in my schedule, I had another excuse to exist another day, so I encouraged them to fill my diary. If I didn't have that, I would've ended it all, no question. When I had music, I had purpose. So, all of my love goes out to them for sticking by me and believing in me when I couldn't believe in myself.

To this day, I still can't shake off the emotional scars of my experience with nefarious and fraudulent characters, and 'he-who-must-not-be-named'. I took all of the hatred and negative emotions I harboured towards this time in my life and transformed them into a positive learning experience, with songs I am really proud of, like 'Honest Men'. I have learnt my lesson and moved on. If karma is a thing, I'll let her do my dirty work for me.

Love Song

I heard it on the radio, in all the stories I've been told
in every phrase and every note. But I don't know.
I see it in the strangers eyes, as they share each others
lives. With roses and with lullabies but I don't know

'Cause I have, never written a love song.
And no-one knows where they come from.
until they come along
And sometimes something saves you or someone
then you can write them a love song, a truly honest one
and maybe this is one

I got lost and couldn't find, the heart of me that beats
inside. ~~with roses and with~~ ~~lullabies~~
So I drew these compass lines, now I'm alive
See I forgot the reasons why. forgot the way two lovers
lie. Hold each other through the night, now I'm alive.

I hear the choirs and I hear the music and
that's why I'm singing for you. I hear the choirs
and I feel the music that's why I'm singing for you

Chapter Seven

LOVE SONG

"It is better to have loved and lost than never to have loved at all."
Tennyson's beautiful quote unfortunately means nothing to me. I have
never been in love. In my 24 years (and counting) on this planet, I have
never once been able to look deep into someone's eyes and tell them I love
them. Of course, I have been in relationships. Two, to be exact. Though
I loved them both at the time, I was never in love with them. Perhaps I
uttered those magical three words in the faint hope that I'd believe it was
possible that someone like me, with all my complexity, could do something
as simple as fall in love?

For much of my pre-adolescent years I was utterly convinced that I was asexual. I just didn't understand sex and affection. When close friends talked about their crushes and the feelings they possessed for some boy or girl, I felt like an alien. I understood physical beauty, but I appreciated it the same way I appreciated a piece of art. Aesthetically pleasing but nothing else. It wasn't until I was 15 that I discovered what it felt like to *desire* someone, *want* someone, as more than just a friend. They didn't look like how I'd imagined they would, which, at first, I struggled with. I fancied a girl. And not just any girl – one of my best friends. Her name was Josephine. Though, to protect her identity, it's not her real name.

I knew I liked Josephine more than just a friend. I rejected the idea that we could be more until a certain trip. She was going to be there, along with all my other friends. The trip was memorable for another reason too – it was the second time I ever got drunk. In those days, it didn't take much. But on this particular night, a one-litre bottle of cider was my weapon of choice. Classy. There came a point in the evening, after having spent a lot of the night together laughing and playfully touching, that consequently, Josephine ended up in my room. At the end of a giggle fit, we both exhaled with joyous exhaustion. Our breath hung in the air and in the moment of silence, she brushed a strand of hair from my cheek. With her fingertips lingering on my face, we both leaned in and kissed. My first ever kiss with a girl. After we kissed, one thing led to another and I had my first sexual experience. I realised then how natural it was to be with another woman. As with most first experiences of this nature, it still felt more than a little awkward afterwards, but I never felt strange about being with a girl.

Obviously, this experience led to a lot of confusion… at a time when I was already very confused about who I was. Was I gay? Did touching and kissing one girl count as being gay? I kept these questions to myself. When other kids in school found out – I never found out how – it obviously led to quite a bit of name-calling. When we spoke about it a few weeks later, she put it down as being a "drunk mistake". I didn't allow myself to be upset about it. In a way, I was grateful. Josephine had taught me something about myself that it may have taken me years to figure out. I now identify as bisexual and enjoy the look and love of both men and women. Though, I fear because of this – or maybe despite it – neither will ever truly love me back.

Headlines

Not long after my experience with Josephine, a new face had started sitting at the 'rejects table' in the food hall. I'd seen him occupying corners in the school corridors. In some way, this stranger had seemed like a mirror of my past self, hiding away from their class mates and making home in the empty spaces of the school building. This boy rarely spoke but when he did, it was meaningful. I was too afraid to speak to him myself. I had to get to know him through the conversations the table held at lunchtime. When he did talk to me, my face would blush and I'd feel light-headed. I could never converse in coherent sentences and rambled on like a babbling buffoon. He must have liked me, despite my awkwardness, as we ended up starting a relationship. This relationship taught me a lot. I learnt that I was neither gay nor straight. After we broke up, I began identifying as bisexual. My sexuality was never something I thought twice about and I never believed there'd be any consequences to me being open about this fact. I was wrong.

My bisexuality made headlines – *headlines!* – in Irish newspapers. I was 18. I had told my fans online the day before and the press picked up on it. Why would I ever think anyone would want to write about this? When the news broke, I was back home in Ireland for the weekend. I was out enjoying a horse riding lesson that evening when my mother returned to the stables to take me home. She had changed. She was angry. Luckily, I was wearing my helmet because she hit me on the head with the *Belfast Telegraph*. "Would you like to explain this?" she shouted. I looked at the paper, the biggest in Northern Ireland. The headline read "Janet: I'm bisexual; X Factor Star Admission. Devlin says she 'swings both ways'."

Even I was shocked by that headline. I didn't expect the physical hit though. Especially from my Mum. As she stormed off she said, "What on God's earth is your grandmother going to say about this? You're going to give her a heart attack!" I stood there for a moment. I couldn't move because of the shock. My Mum already knew I wasn't straight, I had told her years before though I think she thought it was a phase that I'd just grow out of. When I caught up with her in the car, she was cold and distant. I was confused and disappointed. This was the first time I'd felt truly unloved and unaccepted by her. "Your personal life doesn't have to be public, you know!" There was strong aggression in her voice as she drove off. I said nothing. I turned my body to the window. Trying my best to not absorb her anger,

nor radiate mine. In this moment, what tore me up the most was how she accepted my brother, an openly gay man, but not me. We made a stop at Gortin's local supermarket and it was there that I broke my silence. With a Pot Noodle in one hand I turned to her. "So, it's fine for one of your children to be gay but when the other is bisexual, there's suddenly a problem? I think you're being unfair, unreasonable and judgemental!" I may have said this a little too loud. She was standing at the other end of the aisle. I could see panic wash over her face. Before she could shush me, I made my way to the till, paid and waited in the car. Later that night, an apology came. It was rough around the edges. According to her, she accepted my bisexuality, but was still concerned about what others might say. Apparently, my new "fame" after my stint on *The X Factor* warranted her to treat my brother and me differently. She wanted to protect me from the prejudices and bullying of others. I didn't forgive her that day. But I did eventually. My mother loves me unconditionally and that's all that matters.

Love Online

After my three-year relationship with a boy ended – my longest and happiest so far – I struggled to date. By struggled, I mean I didn't date. At all. For four years I was as single as one could possibly be. There were numerous reasons for this. One, I couldn't cope with being touched. I would freeze up in fear if someone grazed my arm or gave me a hug – another infliction inherited from my Dad, perhaps. Two, no one ever asked. I had the odd stranger sending me direct messages over the internet, but that doesn't count. In four years, no one flirted with me in the real world. No guys I met ever offered to go out for dinner or coffee. I came to terms with the fact that falling in love was just never going to be my reality. Truth be told, I had no friends, no social life and I worked all the time. If I were going to meet someone, it'd be through music, or the music industry. Sure enough, my second big relationship was with a photographer I'd once worked with. He asked me out for a coffee and, thinking it was work related, I agreed. We were together for a year, but it ended when I was 22. That relationship taught me that I could be loved – it was possible!

After that, I began dating online. Not something I ever thought I would do – too many *X Factor* questions, too many idiots – but it was something that I actually enjoyed. I may not be good at group socialising at parties, but I do very much enjoy talking to people one-to-one. Though I never found 'the one' on Tinder, I did acquire many hilarious anecdotes. In total, I went on 14 dates. I never told any of them what I did for a living. I'd just say I wrote songs, poetry and edited videos for a living. When asked if that was enough to live on, I'd laugh and say, "By some miracle, it puts bread on the table!" If they probed for more answers, I kept things incredibly vague. It worked. Until the day it didn't.

Around this time I dated a girl, and, as it turns out, her entire friendship circle knew who I was – but she had no idea. She found out when she sent her friends a picture of us together. Their

response meant I had a lot of explaining to do, beginning with: "Yes, that was me on *The X Factor*."

Probably the worst case of getting caught out in this respect was with a guy who I shall name 'Jon' for the purpose of this story. One because he looked like Jon Snow from *Game of Thrones*, and two because I don't want to include his real name.

For our first date, a few years ago, we agreed to go bowling. As a non-drinker, there's not a lot of options when it comes to socially acceptable non-alcohol infused activities. The date went well, he was very lovely, so we agreed to see each other again. We met in Cambridge so we could explore the city and take the time to get to know each other. We decided we'd try punting on the river. I'd never done it before, so I was a mixture of nervous and excited. When we clambered into the boat, I could feel myself being watched by one of the other nearby punters. I didn't think anything of it until all of a sudden this man jumped onto our boat.

Jon and I sat at the end of the boat, facing our new friend. Immediately, this man said: "Are you Janet Devlin?" Jon was shocked that this man knew me by name. As we continued down the river, the punter told us that he watched my new YouTube video releases every Saturday, he had all my albums and singles and that he'd been a massive fan for years! Poor Jon. The penny dropped. After sharing a selfie with this pleasant punter, I turned to Jon with an embarrassed expression and awkwardly told him the truth about who I was and why I never told him I was a singer-songwriter on YouTube (I was too humble to tell him about *The X Factor*). Shocked, and a little upset I hadn't told him, it wasn't long before our city break was back on track. (I was even stopped a few more times by strangers for photos. Luckily, Jon was in the bathroom for one of those!)

After walking around for hours, we finally grabbed dinner. As soon as we were seated, I could feel eyes on me. My suspicion was proved correct when our waiter came to take our order. "Some customers at another table have a question," he began. "Are you Janet Devlin... from *The X Factor*?" Another piece of information I hadn't told my date. Now I had to explain that story too.

Jon took it all well and was very sweet about the whole situation and we went on to laugh about it. Sadly, though, Jon and I never met again. I put this down to not being open with him in the first place. The true reason for this is my belief that knowledge is power. Everyone loves to have a little internet-stalk of their upcoming Tinder date. I didn't want someone to already know more about me than I them before we'd even met.

So, the swiping right continues. As does the hope that 'the one' will sweep me off my feet. Maybe one day I'll meet the person I'm supposed to be with forever. Or maybe I should just buy all the cats and call it a day. Either way, for now, I'm channelling the love I do have back into myself and those I care about. Until then, I'll just keep on singing love songs...

Big Wide World

Sun is rising in the city. On a roof top feelin' dizzy
Don't look down 'cause you're ready now
feelin' nervous but you can do this, this is a place with
no excuses. Don't back down, 'cause you're ready now.

'Cause you've got the pulse, pulse of the city
Flow through your veins. there's no more limit
look to the sky, this town has no ceiling
don't back down...

Welcome to the big wide world, it's bigger than you've
ever heard. It's all you've ever wanted, so we should go
get lost in the big wide world. The big wide world.
The big wide world.

Feel the glow of the streetlight. let your hair down
at midnight don't stop now. live life loud.

'Cause you've got the pulse, pulse of the city. Flow
through your veins, there's no more limit. look to the
sky this town has no ceiling. Don't back down.

Welcome the the big wide world. it's bigger than
you've ever heard. It's all you've ever wanted, so we
should go get lost in the big wide world.

Chapter Eight

BIG WIDE WORLD

In 2011, I felt euphoria for the first time. And it came at the most unexpected moment. It was a dry, brisk autumn morning in central London. I'd been awake since 5 a.m. doing the rounds of breakfast TV. I'd just been eliminated from The X Factor *and it was a rite of passage to recount your experience of the show on as many TV sofas as would have you. It's quite possibly the oddest experience in the world.*

One day I was a student. The next, my face and voice were beamed into the homes of millions of people. I began receiving affectionate tweets from Courtney Love, who gave me permission to sing Nirvana songs for the live show. They even put my name on the front cover of *NME*. It's a truly life changing experience to be plucked from a regular life and dropped into one that demands long working hours, a new living environment and to be surrounded by a bunch of strangers 24 hours a day. Not bad for a little emo kid from Gortin, right?

For the six months in 2011 that I lived and breathed all things *X Factor*, I was scheduled to be at rehearsals or filming pretty much every moment of every day. It was rare to get any more than a few hours' sleep a night. I was fully aware that I'd signed away my right to complain. All I had to do was make it through a few months and that was it. Besides, the switch wasn't so hard for me, as I was fresh from school, a teenager. I was accustomed to asking permission for everything and being told what to do. Pretty soon after my first audition, it became normal not to be able to speak to my friends and family when I wanted to. It was normal to be told when to eat, shower and sleep.

When I got kicked off the show, it didn't immediately sink in that things had changed. I assumed I would go back to life as normal. But the morning I did my first press junket after my departure, it became clear that my life had drastically changed once again. As I sat on the top floor of the ITV building, the sunshine poured in through the glass walls of the large room I was in. It was empty except for me and two other people. The journalist was running late so I had some time to kill. I wanted to go stand on the outside terrace for a moment, and feel the heat of the sun. Not thinking twice, I asked the minder whose job was to look after me for the day if it was OK for me to go outside. I was met with a perplexed look. "Of course, you can!" she said as if taken aback that I'd ask something like that. As I stepped outside and shut the door behind me, I felt embarrassed for asking. As I approached the ledge of the terrace, a feeling hit me at the same time as the sun's rays. My mind raced. I no longer had to ask anyone's permission. I was free. Free from a schedule, a TV crew and constant supervision. My mind was overwhelmed with possibilities. I looked out upon the vast London landscape and let the feelings sink in. In that moment, I was overcome with what can only be described as genuine euphoria. To know that I had a whole lifetime ahead of me to do whatever I wanted, to be whatever I wanted and to live however I wanted was truly mind-blowing. I had escaped a life of pressure and expectation. I felt truly alive for the first time in my life. I could go back to my regular existence if I so wanted, or I could continue to pursue my dream of making music. Of course, I chose the latter but in that moment I was given the choice to do so. The freedom to choose was all that mattered. All the things that had been overwhelming in the last few months melted away like ice cream on a summer's day. As I turned my thoughts to my musical career, the sense of ecstasy only continued. I now had the chance to become the artist I'd always dreamed of becoming and not live a vision of someone else's interest. Images of dream studios and writing rooms flashed up in my mind's eye. I knew that I'd no longer have to write songs in the cold shed at home. That it was now attainable for me to actually begin making my first ever album. I thanked my lucky stars for the opportunities *The X Factor* had given me but I was also thankful to no longer be tied to it.

Everything in this sun-kissed moment was perfect. I was awake. This was a huge shift in perception for me, because at the time I was on prescription medication to help fight severe depression. Though the pills shut up the suicidal thoughts in my brain, they also stopped me from experiencing pure, unreserved happiness. I was trapped in emotional bubble wrap. If I felt the true highs, then the lows would be excruciatingly low. They wouldn't allow me to write a poem let alone a song. Not that I had much time for writing on the show anyways.

After that moment on the roof, I stopped taking all my medication. I missed the feeling of feeling too much. I knew that if the thoughts came back I would start taking it right away. But until then, I was going to be emotionally present again. I never thought this revelation would've been visible to anyone but myself, but I was wrong. When the journalist who came to interview me finally arrived, he commented upon how positive I was. I actually ended up giving the most animated interview of my life so far.

Half the World Away

The best and worst thing about emotions is that they are only temporary. All feelings are fleeting. Happiness can never be truly encapsulated and held onto forever, nor can the low of the bottom be eternal either. A reassuring thought to me as I have done more than my fair share of hitting rock bottom in my life. Looking back now, I wouldn't change it for the world though because even though the lows destroyed me, the highs, though they were few and far between, were enough to keep me alive. But the euphoria that hit me in 2011 was all but gone when January 2015 came

around. Without a doubt, I'd have to say that this was my darkest period. The bottom of rock bottom. Though lots of exciting things were going on in my life, I couldn't see past the darkness. I'd just signed to OK! Good Records in the US and I was excited about the prospect of having my songs released in the States. Despite my dependence on alcohol being at an all-time high at that point – I was using drink as a fast-forward button to skip through the boring bits – the excitement of my first ever showcase gig in America was all-consuming. In the UK, I was alone and depressed and drunk. America gave me hope.

My whole life I'd wanted to go to New York City. And now, after all the downs of my career to date, here I was… about to get on a plane. I couldn't believe that not only was I going there but I was going out there for 'work'. Honestly, if it hadn't been for that trip, I know for sure I wouldn't be here today. After *Running With Scissors* was released in the UK in 2014 and I'd done all the promotion and marketing we could possibly do, I felt incredibly guilty that we had not achieved the success needed to ensure a second record. My future was full of uncertainty. Again. I remained an emotional and financial burden to everyone around me. Thoughts of suicide had returned. I figured that if I took my own life, no one would have to put up with my behaviour anymore and maybe my suicide would garner some media attention that could help sell more records… and hopefully pay back all the people who had invested in me.

This trip to America, and the gig, threw a spanner in the works. It gave me something other than myself to focus on. Now that I was given a brand new promotion schedule, which I was in charge of, I put my suicide on hold. When I landed at JFK airport on a frosty Valentine's Day evening, I was greeted by the head of the American record label, Jurgen, one of my favourite people to this day. Instead of sending a car, or an assistant, it meant a lot that he actually picked me up personally. Not only that though, as it was Valentine's Day, he also brought me flowers, Hershey's Kisses and a balloon. I was taken aback. I didn't deserve someone being so kind. I assumed, I thought, that this new person would be "someone else I'd let down, or who was inevitably never going to earn their money or their time back".

To make things even better (or in my case, worse) I was staying in a lovely hotel in Times Square. I could feel myself becoming more alive, the closer we got to the bright neon lights. I was speechless. I spent most of my time gazing at how tall the buildings were and how beautiful it all looked in the snow. I was awestruck.

When I arrived in my hotel room after having a late dinner at the Hard Rock Cafe, I was full of anxiety at how I was ever going to sleep with the time difference, excitement and previous few night's insomnia flowing through my veins. As soon as my head hit the pillow, however, I was out like a light. It was one of the most peaceful night's of sleep I had ever enjoyed. I was awake by 7 a.m., full of energy. Back home, this would have been the time I'd finally be falling asleep. I was obviously elated by the change of location. I was free for the whole day to do what I wanted. The city was effectively shut down, with temperatures dropping to −17° F. It was so cold that the Hudson river had frozen over! I put on four layers of clothing that day along with thermals.

My managers Rick and Adam and my guitar player, Roo, had accompanied me on the trip and we took to the streets of frosty NYC at noon. The wind was so cold that it felt like my face was going to freeze off every time a breeze went by. We walked through Central Park, which now looked like a scene out of a Christmas movie. Every so often a voice from the park's PA system would announce that everyone should go inside every 15 minutes otherwise there was severe risk of frostbite. We made our way through the empty streets to the top of the Rockefeller Center. Very few other people were at the top, which is incredibly rare. We had the whole view of the city to ourselves. I made my way to the edge of the building to look out at the skyline. It hit me. I was awakened again. I felt both insignificant and minuscule but simultaneously invincible. As I looked down at the circuitry of the streets below, all of my woes were nowhere to be found. For the second time in my life, I was standing on top of a building – the first covered in sun, this time covered in snow – and bathed in the euphoria of sheer joy. I knew my purpose for existing and I was going to stick around to fulfil it. I understood then that there is no meaning to life unless we create one. My world was filled with a new brightness. Colours appeared brighter and everything had a new sharpness and clarity. I glanced around to look at Rick and Adam. I was overwhelmed with gratitude to have them there with me. I wanted to do them proud. I wanted to do myself proud. Everything that once overwhelmed me now felt achievable. To this day, when I feel down, I bring myself back to this memory atop 30 Rock. For the rest of the day, I carried this bliss in a bottle with me.

The next day, after doing the rounds of taping performances and interviews, as requested by my new US label, the day came for the showcase gig at the legendary Red Lion venue on Bleecker Street. To say I was petrified would be an understatement. I was so nervous that I couldn't even film for my YouTube vlog. Stage fright is not a new feeling for me, but this was the worst it had ever been. This time I cared. I wanted so much to put on the best show I possibly could. I needed to remind myself and my team why we were all doing this. I couldn't escape the pressure of a new audience though. I didn't know how I would go down in a new country. I sound-checked in front of people having their lunch. When it finally came time to perform, I was so riddled with fear that I had a shot of tequila to take the edge off. I can't say it helped much as I was still a nervous wreck for the entire show. Thankfully, it didn't affect my performance. I interacted with the audience, told a few jokes and sang my heart out. I felt on top of my game. The audience even listened! Despite playing an acoustic set in a small Irish bar on the East Side, the audience liked me enough not to talk through my 12-song set. When I finished a song, you could hear a pin drop. As the last chord of the last song rang out, I was flooded with endorphins. I thanked every person that came individually, meaning every word. It was the gig of a lifetime. The whole trip was a dream come true. For as long as I live I will cherish my memories of my first time in NYC... and cannot wait to return.

Serenity

My life in the music industry has been filled with many amazing moments. These are the times that keep me going when my mind and body get the better of me. They make every ounce of blood, sweat and tears worth it.

One of the most standout moments of my career to date was when the opportunity to sing for the Dalai Lama came along. It was so unexpected. Out of the blue, my mother received a phone call from a stranger. The stranger, a representative for the event that was due to take place in Derry to celebrate the city being awarded City of Culture 2013, told my mother that they wanted me to sing for His Holiness! That I would sing not only to a hall of attendees but also the Dalai Lama himself blew my mind! When my mother passed this news on to me, I didn't believe her. How could I? It was so unbelievable! I thought it was an April Fools' prank in September, and that a local person was messing with me. Over the years, I had read many – if not all – of the Dalai Lama's books, so this gig seemed too good to be true. I told my mother to go ahead and agree to the gig. If it were a hoax, I'd find out soon enough when they failed to provide a schedule for the event. Needless to say, it turned out to be real. I was floored. I couldn't speak, I just cried with happiness.

When the show day rolled around, not only did I get to sing for His Holiness, I also got to meet him. I was taken to Peace Bridge in Derry, with the city's mayor by my side. People speak of an indescribable feeling of serenity when they meet the Dalai Lama. I can confirm that to be true. For when he took my hand as we walked to his car, I was awash with a sense of peace I had never felt before. To this day I still have the beads he gave me that he blessed. I hold them when I'm feeling nervous before a show... which is every show. I never found out why they asked little old me to perform for this event, but I am ever so glad they did.

Soon after my encounter with His Holiness, I was given the opportunity to perform at another life-changing event: the half-time show of the All Ireland Gaelic football final at Dublin's Croke Park. I'd always wanted to go to the stadium, but I never had. Not even as a punter. So, to attend and sing at the same time ticked off two things from the Bucket List! To add even more joy to the pot, I was also allowed to sing an original song too. Pinch me! I took my brother Aaron with me. Aaron was an avid football fan but also doubled up as my Irish tour manager whenever I performed on home soil. I'd taken him to many shows before and he knew exactly what to do. He would help me laugh and joke despite the enormity of the event: singing in front of over 83,000 people on one of Ireland's biggest calendar days. I sang two songs as the season's highlight reel of that year in football played behind me. The moment now exists as a blur in my mind. I sort of remember being there, but not really. The rush I got when it was over, words will never do justice. The day was a fairy tale brought to life. I'll never forget how lucky I am to have the opportunity to do these things.

When speaking about the happiest moments of my life, I can't forget this one: my trip to Dublin to record the *Confessional* album. It was a series of joys, from finding out that I'd be recording the album to the very last moments of its completion. As the first album was such a rushed process, I never got to witness the musicians play on it. This time was different. I was going to be there for every second of Irish fairy dust that was to be made. My producer, manager and I were staying in a glorious four-storey house in the heart of the city and sessions took place in one of the country's most prestigious studios. What more could I ever have asked for! The only thing I remember going wrong was a bottle of soda spilling onto my clothes during the flight. Easily fixed – buy some new ones in Primark and wash the ones I'd taken. So I did. What I could've done without was the minor awkward moment of my producer and manager having to pick my underwear off the floor, as I'd left my clothes to dry on the roof terrace of the house, not knowing that the wind would pick up and blow my delicates everywhere.

The weather in Dublin was glorious. Not that I'd be seeing much of it in the windowless studio, but it added to the evening's walks through the city. When I arrived at the studio for the first day, I could hardly contain my excitement. This was it, it was finally real. After years of waiting for the day to come when I'd finally start recording *Confessional*, it had arrived. I was not going to take any moment for granted. I also wasn't going to let anything slip by me either as I knew how easy it would be to get caught up in all the fun and lose track of what was going on.

I found a clipboard, some clean sheets of paper and printed out the schedule for the week. I wrote out what tracks each musician needed to play on and even made notes on the extra ones they played on too, writing down which takes had magic in them and which didn't. Basically, if we did anything, I wrote it down, not wanting to miss a single note of anyone's pieces. It was a side of myself I'd never seen before. I don't think I've ever been so organised in all my life and people noticed. Amid my new dictator-style rule of the studio, I still managed to have the time of my life. I can't explain how amazing it is to hear a musician lay down a magic take of your own song. There's a sort of electricity in the control room that words will never do justice to. I was literally jumping with joy and exclaiming with happiness every time a player smashed it. With every track they brought a new dimension, something that cannot be recreated with any plug-in – the sound of a living breathing human. The album finally sounded alive.

Those moments I had in Westland Studios will forever stay with me. I had the time of my life making the album I'd always dreamed I'd make with a team of people I love dearly. I can't believe this is my job. I'll forever thank my lucky stars to have been so blessed.

Away with the fairies

I'm in ribbons again. Can you help me my friend?
I've been searching for my mind but I can't seem to
find it. No matter where I've wandered.
Two sheets to the wind, I'll set sail from my sin
and I'll journey through the night, into the darkness
into the black and into the forests

Grant me wings tonight. Grant me wings to raise me high
Grant me wings tonight. Grant me wings so I can fly.

I'm away with the fairies, I'll be a moonbeam child
I'm away with the fairies, I'll be the banshee cry
Stop holwing. Stop howling, Stop howling out my name
I'm away with the fairies. I'm away, I'm away, away again.

There's a bottle of ghosts. And the horror it hosts
I've been hiding under tables drowning in the fables.
A coffin in a cradle.

Grant me wings tonight. Grant me wings to raise me high
Grant me wings tonight. Grant me wings so I can fly

I'm away with the fairies, I'll be a moonbeam child
I'm away with the fairies, I'll be the banshee cry
Stop howling. Stop howling. Stop calling out my name
I'm away with the fairies. I'm away, I'm away
away again.
I call it a blessing. You call it a curse. My soul is
confessing my life in a verse. I call it a blessing.
You call it a curse, my soul is confessing my life in
a verse.

Chapter Nine

AWAY WITH THE FAIRIES

At the height of my drinking, at aged 18, I was invited to perform on Channel 4's Sunday Brunch. *Then, and today, the show was one of the nation's most popular weekend breakfast TV shows. It was an incredibly big deal for me as it was rare they ever had artists like me do the show. I promptly agreed to do it. But, naturally, it didn't all go to plan... and the moment remains one of my biggest professional regrets to date.*

It was a simple task, really – perform a track and do a quick plug for the release of my debut album, *Hide & Seek*. In my mind I had planned to have a drink on the Friday, be hung-over on the Saturday and do the show on the Sunday. This was not to be the case. On that Friday evening, after I polished off an entire bottle of red wine, I decided it would be a good idea to go sit in the nearest bar for another and then come home. This seems like an odd thing to do but I reiterate: I was incredibly lonely. I wandered down the street to the nearest pub, sat down with my cheapest beer and relaxed. Halfway through the evening, a guy came over to have a drink with me. He seemed rather normal, so I allowed him to sit. We chatted about nothing in particular and his friends would occasionally come over and join us. For some reason these people were giving me free drinks. I can't recall very much of what happened next. I have a brief memory of being in the guy's car on our way to another bar nearby where another group of his friends were. I should've gone home but, by this point, I was blackout drunk. I remember seeing a butterfly logo as we pulled up to the bar. The next thing I remember is waking up in bed next to him. I panicked. What happened? Where was I? Did I sleep with him? A very important question to my strict Catholic conscience. Before I had even the chance to answer that embarrassing question he had already reassured me that we hadn't. Relief was an understatement. To this day I hope that this was the truth and that nothing actually did happen. I've never had a flashback of the night, so even my memory can't be trusted. The guy seemed genuine and I suppose that's why I trusted him. I was offered a lift home and I took it, just happy to be out of there.

When I got back that afternoon, I was so overwhelmed with guilt and shame I continued drinking. I didn't even pay heed to what day it was. I was too busy suppressing my feelings from the morning and night before. The living room of Rick's house, where I was living at the time, had been laid out with a blow-up mattress, as the band were staying over so we could all go to *Sunday Brunch* together. This detail completely slipped my mind. I'd forgotten that I was supposed to leave the key out under a plant pot. The band showed up after midnight. I'd passed out in the living room. I was intoxicated and confused when I heard them knocking. I let them in, muttered a few words of drunken nonsense and made my way to bed. How I even managed to wake up the next morning is beyond me. My alarm went off at 4.30 as a car was to pick us up at 5. I had that feeling of being both drunk and hung-over at the same time. Now, when I say hung-over, this is in no way comparable to the hangover you have after a few too many beverages with your friends in the bar. This was an alcoholic's hangover. I'd been drinking for days and had not eaten or hydrated in God knows how long. I was broken. My hands were shaking, I was sweating profusely, and my body felt like death. I was trying my best to be normal and sober but I knew that this was going to be one of the hardest days of my life. By every fault of my own.

In the bathroom, my body was unable to keep down the toxicity of the past few days. I had no idea how I was going to make it through. I showered, trying to wash off the shame and guilt and in the faint hope it'd make me feel human. It didn't. When it came to brushing my teeth, my gag reflex was off, so I stood there, dry heaving for a good 10 minutes. Finally, we left the house. The band didn't say very much, there was nothing they could say. But they were concerned, not only for me, but for our appearance in front of the nation live on TV. Every ounce of my energy was focused on being OK. Trying to walk, trying not to shake and what felt like trying not to die. I clambered into the car and fell asleep. I woke up in the parking lot of the television studio, feeling even worse than before. It appeared that the more I sobered up, the more pain I was in.

When I finally arrived at the dressing room I lay down in the foetal position. I wasn't needed for a while. By this point all I had to do was wait for my call to be in make-up, put my dress on and then wait for my cue to go live. It was obvious to everyone that something was wrong. My team whispered and tried their best to figure everything out. This was a disaster. My band feared the worst, my publicist was in shock and Adam was shaking with worry. I'm not sure what actually went on in that dressing room. I heard a few guys discussing that day's football match as I tried with all my might to sleep. After what felt like forever, I was finally called into make-up, had my outfit on and was ready and waiting. In my confused state, I forgot to do the make-up for my arm. The scars I had from a fresh bout of self-harming were red raw and aggressive. I'd usually cover them with thick layers of concealer. So, there I was, on a Sunday morning, sat in front of the nation in the most pain of my life. I tried my best to smile and fake my way to the end of the show. My introduction had been made and it had been stated that I'd be playing the show out later. A fake copy of my album was shown and the presenters plugged it. Later on, in the food segment of the show, I was offered some of the dishes that were cooked on air. I had to politely decline as I feared even the smell of food was going to set off my gag reflex again. I was waved to take my place in another part of the studio for my performance. How this was going to play out, I had no idea! I could barely move without severe internal pain, never mind sing! The music started and so did I. I made it through the song. I think that's the best that can be said about my performance. I could feel the band's relief in the air. Everyone from my team was just glad that it was over. We could all finally head home, and this day could finally end.

I'd worried everyone that day, not just my team but strangers on set. David Baddiel (the famous UK comedian and fellow guest on the show) was so concerned about my health that he personally asked Rick if I was all right, enquiring specifically about the scars on my arm. I did not, however, acquire this knowledge until later on in the day. I had survived public scrutiny this time, I think, but my mother saw the *Sunday Brunch* appearance and, alarmed, came to visit. I wanted to be OK for her, but I wasn't. I couldn't stay sober for her time with me. Of course, like any mother, she was distraught. There was nothing she could do. Every avenue was being exhausted from a parenting angle. Being kind and loving didn't work and nor did yelling. Unfortunately, she was starting to get yelled at herself. When I couldn't keep it together my manager and my mother would have disagreements. When I think of all the blame my Mum got for how I was, it tears me apart. All she ever did was love me. I know it sounds cliché, but she was, and is, the best Mum in the world. To this day when people blame the parents for how their children turn out, it makes my blood boil. I am to blame for whatever happens, and the consequences...

Bottom of the Bottle

Not for the first time, and far from the last, I realised my addiction to alcohol could no longer be ignored. It was September 9, 2014, a Tuesday. I had spent that summer drinking myself to near death across occasions too many to count. It was on the evening of the official release of *Destiny* (the video game, the beta test) that rock met bottom.

I was over the moon to be invited to such an event, of course, a satisfying knock-on effect of my time on *The X Factor*. Life was becoming somewhat of a drunken abyss by this point, counter-weighted with the touring, performing, press, recording, and of course bouts of songwriting and rehearsals that kept my professional life afloat, even if my personal life was sinking underneath. I loved my life, I loved the irregularity of it, the wild unpredictability, but being a musician when you are facing internal demons that threaten to drown your creativity becomes unsustainable, quite quickly. I had a drink for every autograph I wrote. When I try to recollect any great details of specific events surrounding this period of my life, I come to a wall. I try hard to remember but nothing comes back to me – I know where I ended up but how I got there remains unknown. So, the exact reason for why I was drinking that September Tuesday, I'm unaware of. I had a recording session in the morning, I remember that, but I was still drunk from the night before. I managed to make it to the studio at my producer Graeme's house, but I was in no position to sing. When I drink, I lose the ability to sing, or write music. Whatever focus or control I'd usually apply to carry a tune dissipates with

a drop. Hence why I've never done a show with more than one drink in me – something I am proud of, even if the first thing I turned to after a show was drink.

As soon as I arrived at Graeme's house, he called it a day. He was far to kind to me on that day, and all subsequent days, during that time of excessive drinking, and somehow he'd still continued to work with me. But he knew then the path I was on. He sat me down and tried to talk sense to me, but I was adrift, and he knew.

When I left the studio, I went straight to the off licence. I drank more than usual for the daytime and faster than before. I like to think that something inside of me knew that this was going to be the day I hit the bottom, and so I tried to sneak in a few more drinks to soften the blow. How I was going to be red carpet ready for the *Destiny* premiere, just a few hours away, was beyond even my own comprehension. I somehow managed to get home, get dressed and make my way to the tube station. The line between topped up enough to function and full-on drunk had been crossed. I was drinking gin straight from the bottle on the train, not caring who stared at me or for how long. But, for whatever reason, the booze wasn't hitting me the way it usually would; the effects weren't coming quick enough to pacify me. This led to me drinking faster on the train. By the time I arrived at King's Cross Station, I blacked out. The bottle was empty.

My next memory is being stood outside the bathrooms at King's Cross with police officers asking me questions I didn't want to answer. People stared. Rightfully so. I was trying to explain that I was meeting someone, and I had somewhere to be, contrary to the fact that they'd just found me asleep in the toilets. Just as I could no longer hold my head up, I could see MJ, the digital music manager at my management company, entering the station. I pointed, assuring the police officers "That's him, that's him! That's MJ, he's picking me up. Can I go now?" Poor MJ swept me off my feet before I collapsed, with the promise to the police officers that I was to be taken straight home.

My next moment of coming to was in MJ's car. I was crying my eyes out and pleading with him not to take me back to Rick, my manager's home, where I was staying indefinitely. "Why do you do this to yourself?" asked MJ, concerned but also disappointed. I didn't know the reasons why. I didn't know if I was all right either. I don't remember getting home, I don't remember coming to and I don't remember how it made me feel. I wish I could say I felt shame, guilt and remorse, but they weren't penetrating the surface. I felt nothing because I was exhausted from feeling everything. Rick couldn't find the words but hugged me and ensured I got to my room OK. He told me later that he checked on me every 15 minutes to make sure I was still breathing and hadn't choked on vomit.

As I slowly scratched my way to recovery in bed, calls were being made to my press team. They had to be told what happened so as to avoid it coming out in the press or online. This is what they call 'damage control'. They all prayed that there were no photographs of me outside King's Cross, collapsed. These photos can kill careers. I managed to get out of it unscathed from a PR perspective. It never became public knowledge – until now – thank God. I always think I came this close to losing it all. I was a role model to the fans who were starting to listen to me as an artist, my dream, but my halo had slipped off completely. I was an alcoholic at 19 years young. I needed to get help. Again.

12-Step Blues

I was five years old when I felt the first burn of whiskey at the back of my throat. It tasted like fiery pitchforks, stabbing the back of my mouth. It set the pit of my stomach aflame as it scorched the lining. It was wretched. I would never in a million years have thought that, only a few years later, I would come to enjoy – *need* – that burn more than the taste of food. And, as I came to learn, the burn of any alcohol would fuel me; I had grown fond of all flavours. It would be another decade before I tasted alcohol again (save for the thick froth of my father's Guinness every now and again), at my best friend's 16th birthday party. I got drunk to talk to a boy, the same boy I would hide my *X Factor* audition from.

Following my downfall at the Cross of Kings, my team of angels (Rick and my press team) stepped in and asked for me to seek help. I'll stop short of calling it an intervention, as I can't quite bring myself to say it out loud. They suggested I attended a scheme for alcohol management. I didn't fight them. I was outnumbered. Two days later, I was at a government sponsored programme for alcoholics at a secular building, renowned locally for being the home of 'alcoholics' and 'druggies'. I had no expectations or illusions; this was the underbelly that the world had tried so hard not to show me and protect me from. Rick came with me. I made my way to the front desk and with a quick and concise conversation, I was told to sit down and wait, that someone would be with me shortly. I did as I was told. As I waited, submerged in my thoughts of embarrassment, awkwardness and sheer terror, I barely noticed a fight break out in the corridor. One of the men seemed only to have rage on his mind. The other was trying to console him. "How had it come to this?" I thought. But, of course, I knew.

Rick and I sat, frozen still and in utter silence, watching the 10-minute long argument unfold. The yelling was broken when I heard the lady at the front desk call my name. I quickly made my way to the desk and was greeted by a tall, friendly man called Tom. Tom escorted me to a room only accessible with a key fob. The room was terrifyingly simple. Just two padded seats, sat opposite each other in a space not much larger than a cloakroom. "So, what brings you here today?" he asked. I was stunned with how open ended the question was. It sent my mind racing with all the intricate life choices I had made, hoping to find one event that would sufficiently answer his query. After a nodded prompt from Tom, I answered, "I think I have a problem". As I'd just pointed out the elephant in the room I re-examined my answer and tried again. "I have an alcohol problem... I'm an alcoholic." With that he shifted, as if he'd not expected the term alcoholic to fall from my mouth. This prompted a series of questions regarding how much I drank, how often I drank and why I drank. It appeared that I ticked all the boxes. As quickly as the assignment had begun I had already enrolled into a group class for 'alcohol management'.

"Have you ever been to any classes for help with your alcohol before?" Tom inquired as he passed me the forms for my signature. I noticed he had self-harm scars on his arm, mostly covered by bracelets. It took me by surprise as he didn't fit my prejudices of what a self-harmer looked like. I explained my incident in London as my reason for attending the meeting. "It's for the best," he responded, looking shocked.

To be accepted into my class of alcohol control, I had to guarantee that I would attend every Monday at 11 a.m. for one hour for eight weeks. In other words, I was in hell.

A Major Minor

When that first Monday finally rolled around I was terrified. I had been up drinking from the night before and somehow managed to top up that morning too. I was passible drunk. "Functioning" as they called it. It was a 10-minute walk from my manager's house, where I was still allowed to stay, to my first class.

As I rang the doorbell at the centre, someone shouted abuse from their car window when the traffic light went green. "Junkie scum", I heard. It was official, I was in *Trainspotting*.

Inside the building, every moment I was in the waiting room was a moment too long. The therapies were confined and sorted to those of the sexes. "You ladies can go on through," a woman said as she held open the door to the back. We went further down the corridor this time, arriving at a large room filled with natural light. It had huge tables, a kitchen and a white board. The walls were filled with motivational posters and photographs of adults on what appeared to be class trips. At this point in my life I'd stopped questioning things. I just did what I was told to do, sat where I was told to sit and tried my best to listen. I was drunk at a class. I'd already broken the rules.

We started off with silly get-to-know-you games. A stress ball was thrown around the room and we'd state our name and a 'fun fact' about ourselves. I assumed that "I'm Janet and I drink myself to sleep because suicide is socially unacceptable" was, in fact, a socially unacceptable thing to say. I refrained. It felt patronising but also necessary. If I'd been willing to sober up, I'm sure these tactics would've worked. For when you're in active addiction, you almost become a child. So, the activities of "What would you pack in your suitcase for a holiday versus what would you pack for sobriety?" though over simplified, may actually work for some. Not for me.

By no fault of the programme, I stayed drunk. Out of the six classes, I attended four sober. Something in it must've been working though. Every week I'd be asked to write down my aim or goal for the coming week. I quickly noticed that every task involved pleasing people. "Stay sober to make my Mum happy" and "Make everyone worry less" and "Show my team that I want this". I almost graduated that class. I say almost because I had to go home before week seven. My manager was going on honeymoon and with my past of being on my own, no one could trust me to be left to my own devices. I'd been advised to take the month off back home in Ireland. I didn't disagree with this suggestion. It did,

however, terrify me. I'd never taken longer than a few days off since my career kick-started in 2011. The idea of slowing down was petrifying to me. I also carried a lot of shame about going back. I didn't want to be seen as a failure to those around me. Though this was all projected insecurity, it was all too real in my own mind. My mother, who always expected the next call she'd get about me would be the one informing her of my death, lived each day with my illness. If I was going to change, it would be for her. But that time wasn't now.

Sweet Sacred friend

Every night I'm running home so we can finally be alone
and I'll lock the door, no world, no more.
Oblivious your middle name and every time I called, you came.
And you held me tight and said goodnight.

You tasted like home. But no one could know.

fare thee well sweet sacred fried who I hope to never see
again. It was a blessing in the end. You tore the deamons
from my side you had to fall to give me life sweet
Sacred friend.

Couldn't live without your touch but when your
love became too much then you made me fight
to the death or life. But in this war nobody ~~can~~
won. I lost a friend, the only one who could
till my skin, the void within.

You taste like regret. But I've laid you to rest.

fare thee well sweet Sacred friend who I hope to never
See again. It was a blessing in the end.
You tore the deamons from my side you had to
fall to give me life sweet Sacred friend.

I can hear you calling, oh you're calling out my name
I can hear you calling me again.

Chapter Ten

SWEET SACRED FRIEND

From the onset of early adulthood, I sought solace at the bottom of a bottle. When anxieties ran high and hopes ran low, I found myself consuming copious amounts of liquid poison to get by. My alcoholism started off as an innocent fondness for a substance that could eradicate all ingrained social anxieties. But what began as a naive romance slowly descended into a dependence that often tiptoed along the equilibrium of life and death. My only objective became oblivion. I was unable to cope with the everyday.

A lcohol filled a void that I always knew I had – which is apparent in all of my self-destructive behaviours. Unlike its predecessors, though, it hurt more than just me. It tore happiness from everyone I came into contact with. Though my relationship with alcohol was problematic, I do believe that it was in fact my solution. For in the darkest depths of my insanity, this substance actually kept me alive. Not living but alive. The question that I get asked the most is "What was your rock bottom?" The problem was that every time I hit my metaphorical bottom, I just kept digging. Nothing could pry the bottle from my cold, clammy hands. It seemed as though I was waiting for death to do it for me. Not even passing out on the floor of King's Cross station with policemen by my side (on my way to a red carpet) was enough to sober me up.

Now that I consider myself healthier and happier than I've ever been, I can look back and say, without equivocation, that 2014 was the year that changed everything. It was the year I hoped would cement my arrival in the nation's hearts. Of course, it was not to be. As all this unfolded, so did I. The previous 24 months of noise and fame, and touring with *The X Factor*, had left me broken, bruised and burnt out. I was well known but alone. My dream life was becoming a reality; I was doing what I thought God wanted me to do, but the nightmare of my own self-sabotage wouldn't allow me my happiness. My drinking spiralled out of control and old habits came back to haunt me. Bankruptcy, self-harming, pills, binge drinking, suicidal depression, exhaustion, homelessness and dejection – they all came up from the depths to greet me. Yes, 2014 is the year that is hard to remember, but difficult to forget.

Room Service

Of course, the road to the end must always start with a beginning. That point for me came after the X *Factor* tour had finished, at the end of 2012. At a crossroads, like everyone coming off such a huge life-changing experience, I acquired new management and immediately started the writing process for my first record. It was an exciting time to be me. I travelled back and forth from Ireland to England weekly, and found residence in studios and writing rooms, making progress on the biggest dream of my life – an album.

As much as writing the album was exhilarating and exciting, with hindsight, I see now how isolated I truly was. I was unaware, or unable to process it all at the time, but I was as lonely as when I was that stick-thin girl on the school playground two years earlier. Fame hadn't changed me, unfortunately. Now, when the day was done and a song had been written, food wasn't my enemy – loneliness was. I would go back to my hotel room alone. I had no solid base beyond whatever hotel I was staying in for the duration of the sessions. My free time was spent in solitude, in a room that wasn't my own, in a city I was unfamiliar with. I wasn't able to go out on my own and wander aimlessly through city streets. I'd been well warned against that. Not only would I have been an easy target as a lost 17-year-old girl, I also couldn't go anywhere at the time without being recognised. So, I stayed in.

I'd seek companionship on the internet by doing live streams. Sometimes I'd just write poetry and scroll through endless videos online. This eventually became boring. One night after a week of session work in Sheffield I decided that I would treat myself to room service. It was rare that I did this, as it could sometimes be very costly. I pondered on the idea of ordering a glass of the hotel's cheapest red wine with my chicken salad and fries. I was 17, underage, so if they asked for ID I would've felt foolish. Eventually I figured I would chance it – the worst they could say was "no". Thirty minutes later, I heard knocking at my door. I gestured the man towards the end of the bed for him to lay the tray upon it. He then handed me the receipt for a signature. My palms were sweaty. I kept my head down and my penmanship quick. Without a second glance he was gone. A sweet sigh of relief came over me as the door closed. A surge of adrenaline kicked into my system for getting away with it.

This was the beginning of the end. This was the moment where everything slipped southwards.

This was my first time drinking on my own, but it wasn't to be my last. It started with a glass of red wine but quickly became a bottle. Economically justified because it was cheaper that way. I developed my own little ritual. Every last night of session work – usually a Friday – I would order a bottle of wine. I'd found comfort in the structure of it all. I'd sit on my hotel room bed, alone, glass of wine in one hand and smartphone in the other. Eventually I'd scroll myself to sleep. Drunk. This was not the life of a 'normal' teenager.

When this cycle of writing, touring, writing came to an end, and with an album's worth of songs to show for all my hard work, I found myself alone again. But this time in my own flat, a very basic, no-frills apartment. I had little money, earnt from the *X Factor* tour, but what I did get paid I put towards my own independence. But what I thought would be my little safe space actually become the tipping point towards my daily dependence on alcohol. Two of us lived in this little flat, me and my own worst enemy – me.

For the six months I lived on my own, I gradually started to drink more. I didn't see the sadness in it. I'd dance around my bedroom in the early hours of the morning, lip-syncing along to all my favourite songs. Though I was achieving lots in my work life, my personal life was non-existent, and I had acquired zero practical skills. I'd somehow managed to make it this far in life without really knowing how a washing machine worked or how to cook a nutritious meal. I lived on a diet of take-out food, microwave meals, liquor and coffee. Drinking allowed me to be social, have fun, exude a confidence that I hadn't felt since before my eating disorder stripped it away a few years prior. I never exercised or even knew how to look after myself. I put on a show for everyone. I made out as though I was contented, capable and conquering life, but this was not the case. I'd bought into this ideal too, happy to live in denial. Some days I would refrain from getting out of bed at all. I'd wake up in the afternoon, make some food and go back to bed. I was depressed.

As the new year of 2014 emerged, any sign of fresh starts and new beginnings were shattered. I'd hit a personal new low with drinking. This was when I moved out of my flat and into the home of my manager and his fiancé. They were kinder to me than any person could ever deserve, and I repaid them with even more self-destruction.

Within the first few days of being back in England I had already started drinking again. One night I'd taken it so far as to stay up on my own with a bottle of Jack Daniels. I ended up throwing up out of the living room window with much of it ruining Rick's pavement below. I cared enough to be embarrassed, but not enough to stop me from drinking. A mixture of inner turmoil and a fear of not sleeping meant that any night I could drink, I would drink. I reached my breaking point with my inability to sleep. I flew back to Ireland and pleaded with my doctor to prescribe me sleeping pills. Reluctantly, he did. My prayers had finally been answered as for most nights I was able to drift off, almost like a regular person. Though it was a lot less sleep than I required, those three or four hours kept me away from the bottle. Though it wasn't enough to keep me away from my thoughts.

At 18, my self-harm was my main form of avidly acting out at this point. Eventually self-harming alone was not enough to fill my self-destructive void. My regular nightcap consisted of two zopiclone and a £6 bottle of whiskey that I'd pick up from the corner store. I still wouldn't drink every night. One evening, Rick confronted me about my drinking. Since I was living in his home, he could see how much I was consuming. Not even the true extremity of it, as I was doing most of it in secret, and the problematic incidents were still somewhat sporadic. With loving concern, he asked whether I believed alcohol was a problem. I remember my answer as it was later used against me months down the line: "I would never let my drinking get in the way of my work."

For some months this was true; I would never drink the night before a day's work. However, this was a standard that oftentimes fell by the wayside. In late 2013, I began recording my second album, *Running with Scissors*, for Insomnia Music, Rick's management label. Though I never turned up drunk, I do believe my blood would've told a different story. As someone who had zero self-worth or self-belief, I was unworthy of this opportunity with Rick and his team. I had wasted, squandered all my chances so far... why would this be any different?

I commuted from north London to the studio almost every day for weeks. One day I remember being painfully hung-over. I was in all-over pain from the abuse I'd waged upon my body. I clambered onto the train and sat down. I read my email to do list and to my horror I'd not done my 'homework' for the session. It was common practice that I would have something to do in the evenings after a studio session, mostly lyric changes and learning new melodies for existing songs. I'd chosen to cover 'Friday I'm In Love' by The Cure. However, I hadn't learnt my parts for the day. While I was on the train I received a phone call from one of the producers. What should've been a simple and assuring chat quickly became the opposite. When asked if I'd learnt all my parts, I lied and agreed. A simple question set off the panic "Did you have any problems with the middle 8?" to which I stupidly replied, "There's a middle 8?" Anxiously they laughed it off, but I could hear the disappointment and concern in their laughter. The train journey consisted of me listening to the track on repeat. My hung-over brain tried to absorb the song. I'd obviously heard it a million times before but when learning a track, you know this doesn't equate to knowing it. The day was painful. I was somewhat aware of how much I was

unnecessarily inconveniencing everyone, but I couldn't seem to stop it. This only led to a knotted stomach from the pangs of guilt. If I was fully aware of it, I know for certain I would be unable to function. I don't know how anyone was ever able to work with me. I'd turn up as a shadow of a human being, self-harm scars up and down my arms and reeking of the night's consumption.

By no power of my own, the album was finally finished. As if the task of making a record in six weeks wasn't gargantuan enough, try adding an unaware alcoholic in the mix. Next came the mastering of the record. It was to take place in the prestigious Abbey Road Studios. For the first time in a long time, I actually felt something. A foreign feeling that I hadn't had in forever. It was excitement, anticipation with a large portion of anxiety and unreservedness on the side. Any sane rational human being would've gone to bed the night before like a child on Christmas, all tucked up early and ready for the big day. But I was not of sane body or mind so obviously I did the opposite. As aforementioned, I had feelings about this day. Feelings however did not correlate with my state of numbness. Hence my subconscious urge to drown them out. What was unfamiliar had to be stopped. That night I sat up with a bottle of gin and surfed the internet. The misconception that one must be sad to drink is common. I, however, was not sad. By this point, I just drank for the sake of drinking. Hair of the dog was my breakfast – not because I was hung-over and needed it to get by, but because it was left over from the night before, tucked away under my pillow just in case anyone came in. I made my way to the bottom of the bottle and I eventually got ready to head to Abbey Road. I wasn't drunk, I was merely just topping up. Thankfully, when the mastering was done, we all had a celebratory drink. None of this was in any way out of the ordinary. I walked about the studios, glass of wine in hand, looking around a living breathing musical museum. I was overwhelmed with feelings of sheer gratitude. As always, it was a feeling that wouldn't last long…

Holy Water

I bathe in holy water in search of what I've done
I had to share my sorrow and treat it like a son.
Now I feel ten stone lighter with the devil off
my back. I'm cursed to never stumble, I'm cursed
to never crack.

If I ever run away they know where I'll be found
No I can never run away I'm sure they'd hunt me down
but maybe you, maybe you could help to

Wash away my demons and take them
from me. Wash away my demons have mercy
wont you please? Wash away my problems and
send them to the sea. Wash away my demons
and cleanse my inequity. Holy water save me
Holy water save me, yeah save me from me

I'm sorry for the bother, I'm sorry for the sins.
I'm here before your altar I pray that's the end.
And with the voice of reason and with some help
from friends. I hope to one day slumber, I hope
to sleep again.

Chapter Eleven

HOLY WATER

To most people, living a completely sober life sounds like hell. In many ways, it is. I wasn't exactly overjoyed to find out that I could never drink again. In the beginning of my addiction to alcohol, booze gave me things I never thought a possibility if I were sober. I could talk to strangers, be confident and, most importantly, ignore the loud voice of self-hatred ringing incessantly between my ears. Though, ironically, my drinking got so out of hand that come the height of my drinking escapades, I had lost these positive aspects too. When I tell people I don't drink any more I get a mixed response. Some people are shocked. Some people applaud. Everyone asks why.

The assumption that you need alcohol to have a good time is false. As someone who needed to have at least a few drinks before they left the house every day, I can vouch for this. I still go to parties, I still stay out until silly o'clock in the morning and even manage to make questionable life decisions too. All without drink. This life choice has had more pros than cons, to be honest. I never wake up with a hangover. I gain more hours than I know what to do with, hours that are usually wasted recovering from a hangover. The big con? That's obvious. Awkward first dates. But that's a smallish price to pay. I have now been sober for three years.

It is often said when you put down a bad habit, you pick something else up in its place. I'm guilty of this. Thankfully, I threw myself headfirst into my music. And, as always, rather than working at a sensible rate, I instead took my work ethic to a whole new level. I first set my sights upon my YouTube channel. I wanted to create and post more content than ever before. I loved the feeling of uploading. It was a direct hit of dopamine every time I posted. To watch the comments, views and subscribers come in and go up became addictive. I set myself a goal of two videos a week. It doesn't sound like much but when you're already a full time singer/songwriter, it was a pretty big task. Uploading content was benefiting my music career too. It became a very useful promotional tool. When videos went viral, I'd make new fans and subsequently more people began listening to my original music. I even began garnering recognition from the YouTube platform itself, being invited to perform at Google and YouTube events, filming promotional videos for them and becoming a part of creator campaigns.

After my first year in recovery, in 2015, I started to push myself into creative realms that I never had before. I was in such a positive

mindset and my output was so good, that I even asked to take on more projects. Within six months I had written, recorded and released an entire Christmas EP, written, recorded and released a single ('Outernet Song') along with a music video, starred in a movie (*Songbird*) and written and recorded two songs for its soundtrack, edited, filmed and uploaded two videos a week for my increasingly popular YouTube channel, and finished the year with a headline tour around the UK.

On top of all that I made sure I went to a minimum of three addiction meetings a week and maintained a relationship with my then-boyfriend. At the time, I didn't care about where I lived. I was barely there. I had moved out of Rick's house and into a new place in Hertford, with two strangers. I slept on a mattress on the floor in a three-bedroom run-down flat. I survived on a diet of microwave meals and energy drinks. I couldn't afford any luxuries. A far cry from the glamour of the red carpets I once walked during *The X Factor* days and nowhere near the life people assumed I had as a result. It was on that mattress that the concept for the album *Confessional* came to be. Many of my lyrics arrived while living in that little dingy bedroom.

With this new intense work ethic, something had to give. And it did. I relapsed with my eating disorder. What started off as missing a few meals by accident through sheer exhaustion of working long days quickly became a full-blown issue again. I dropped from a healthy 117 pounds to a mere 96 pounds. Obviously, it didn't go unnoticed by friends, family or fans watching my online videos. I was in denial about the affect it was having on me, too. Anorexia played into my plague of a need for perfectionism. I set high standards or goals in hopes that they would feed my self-worth. They never did. I'd set goal weight after goal weight in the belief that once I reached it, I would be happy. It worked for a while. With every job I ticked off my to do list and every pound I lost, I felt euphoric. In my head I was at the peak of productivity. My work and my eating disorder became best friends. I needed a distraction from constantly thinking and obsessing over food and work gave that to me. But after a few months, the bubble burst and I began the journey of recovery again.

I continued to work hard but I also had to look after myself. I moved into a beautiful house in Hertford, this time with a friend of mine, and began building myself back up again. When I felt like I had my demons under control, I began writing this book in 2017. I even found the producer for *Confessional* too, Jonathan Quarmby. I worked hard, hopping from writing session to writing session. I had the basis for 60 songs under my belt and I was still going. The process for writing these songs was something I truly enjoyed and by all means was my favourite form of therapy. I would turn up to a studio somewhere, armed with my books of poetry and I'd begin sharing my story with my songwriting partners and producer, Jonathan. We'd pick a topic and commence writing. Though I wrote some of the songs for *Confessional* completely by myself, I do find co-writing beneficial at times. With someone by your side to keep you focused, you arrive with a set goal and leave with a song most of the time. Also, it stops my perfectionist gene from kicking in. I have people to bounce my ideas off and reassure me that they're good. On my own, I sometimes never finish songs because I can't make them 'perfect'. Also, it's a much more efficient way for me to write; I don't have to spend hours trying to find the chord I can hear in my head, as I can find it in minutes with someone who knows their way around a piano.

The two self-penned songs were 'Holy Water' and 'Honest Men', both of which I wrote in 2018. I remember vividly how 'Holy Water' came to be. I was just a few weeks away from my trip to Ireland to begin recording the album. I'd already written a song under the same name but upon others hearing the album demos, Rick and Jonathan told me that it wasn't up to the same standard as the others. I was fuming. Not because the song wasn't good enough but because no one had said anything until now. I kept my mouth shut as new writing sessions were being discussed for a

replacement song. I got home late that night and stewed over how I felt. When I awoke the next day, I was tasked with completing a book chapter. I ignored this request and grabbed my ukulele. In less than 30 minutes, the 'Holy Water' we now know was written. Whether or not it was any good, I had no idea. I took it to Jonathan the next day. "It's either so simple that it's genius… or… well… crap." We demoed and sent it out to people whose opinion I trusted. Needless to say, they enjoyed it. Despite its subject matter – or maybe because of it – 'Holy Water' is probably my favourite track on the album. From darkness… came light.

Epiphany

For some of the songs I wanted Irish instruments to add a flavour of my home to the record. Rick and Jonathan agreed and called up some session players. We booked a studio in Dublin, one of my favourite cities, to add the final pieces to the puzzle. This week of intense recording was either going to make or break the album. I was ready. I had waited years for this moment and nothing was going to ruin it for me. The only somewhat questionable thing I was doing was popping pills. I was taking modafinil, a eugeroic (a wakefulness-promoting agent used to treat narcolepsy). As previously mentioned, I made copious notes on the day's sessions and would tick off everything on the to-do list, which I had pre-prepared for the trip. I wanted to ensure that nothing got forgotten. I also filmed everything while I was out there. For the first time in my life I felt like I had everything under control and I felt unstoppable. As well as the recording, it was just amazing to be in my home country. When I left, I felt like everything was finally coming together on this project, that all the work I'd done hadn't been in vain and that everything was on the up and up.

Which was true until winter hit again. Gone was the glorious summer of sunshine and long days, replaced in its absence with dark grey clouds that loomed over London. As per every year, my depression came flooding back as quickly as the weather changed. Though I took numerous steps to ease its grasp on my stability, no amount of SAD lamps, meditation or self-care was going to stop the tropical storm that hit my mind. I don't exactly know when I clocked out of feeling things and I wasn't fully aware that I had. With hindsight, I can see things much clearer. I stopped crying at movies, I stopped feeling happy with completing a task and I sure as hell stopped connecting with people. It's very hard to explain those months without emotions. I just sort of existed. I was also starting to have what I can only explain as sober blackouts. I'd forget hours and hours of my life that I'd only realise I'd forgotten when I'd see a photo or a video and realise I had no recollection of being there. I'd be on a date and realise that I hadn't heard a word they'd said in the last 10 minutes (initially I passed it off as just being stressed). My words had left me. It would take me forever to get a sentence out. I'd try to reference a painting or a song that I'd adored for years to someone, only to find that I'd forgotten the name.

Things came to an all-time low by December. I'd begun to abuse sleeping pills to a hellish extent, leaving my memory even more shot and me even more discombobulated. In December 2018, I ordered a bottle of wine to drink alone in my bedroom. With my first swig I realised how futile this substance was. How could I have been so afraid of this for so long. It tasted revolting. I waited for something to happen. An epiphany of emotions is what I expected, but what I got was an empty bottle and a familiar emptiness. I awaited the repercussion of my life falling apart once more. How was I going to pull myself out of this one?

Better Now

Blood stained porcelain, crying on my own again
I'm better now, I'm better now
Once lost, never found. Thank God my thoughts don't
make a sound, 'cause I'm better now

But the truth won't come from empty lungs
but lies will come from everyone.
Can you hear me now? I'm better now.

Glass bones paper skin, just Ghosts within
I'm fading out, I'm fading out
Bruises on white this is the spotlight going down
I'm fading out
But the truth won't come from empty lungs
but lies will come from everyone
Can you hear me now? I'm better now
That all the world is moving on and everything
I've got is gone.
Can you hear me now? I'm better now

Can you hear me?
Can you hear me?
Can you hear me screaming
can you hear me
can you hear me
can you hear me lying...

Chapter Twelve

BETTER NOW

Originally, I wanted to conclude this book with all the positive anecdotes learnt from being sober since June 2015. But that would not have been the truth. It wouldn't have reflected the true ups and downs of my world. In December 2018, I relapsed with alcohol. It was by no means as messy as my prior dances with the drink, but the relapse signified something more symbolic about my life. Just when I think I'm out for good, something pulls me back in. I've learnt the hard way that alcohol is not for me. I'm aware of the consequences and just how horrific it makes me feel. So why did I drink again? After speaking with numerous therapists about this very question, the answer would appear simple. It was a cry for help.

Remaining sober for more than three years only to hit an emotional bottom at Christmas 2018 was not something I had planned, nor had the tools for. On the outside I had everything

I could need: sobriety, friends, family, a boy I liked, and a career doing something I loved. Knowing I should be grateful for this only gave me another stick to beat myself up with. Consequently, my guilt and anxiety led to a one-month stint in a rehab situated in the hills of Ireland. What brought me there was a level of dissociation and depersonalisation that I had never experienced before. Life was something that was happening to me – without me realising. When I was present in the moment, I found myself dreaming of suicide again. I began losing hours of my life, feeling emotionally disconnected and permanently perplexed as to what was going on. I reached for the bottle as a last resort, in the hope that it would bring me back into reality, or at the very least make me feel something. I drank three times in December, each as vacuous an experience as the last.

I'd planned to go sober on January 1 – 'New Year, New Me' and all of that. When I awoke on New Year's Day, I knew this task was too much for me to tackle on my own. I was petrified. I felt silenced by my dilemma. I didn't know who I could confide in, nor did I want to share my shame over what I'd done. Within an hour, I had already booked a flight home and informed mother of my arrival. A few hours later I was in a Starbucks at Stansted airport, googling rehab centres in Ireland. I'd already been in contact with one the day after my first drinking relapse and decided after a bit more research that this was the one I would get in contact with.

After a few emails and a few phone calls it was arranged. I texted my mother: "Hey Mum, I'm sending you this text so that you know what's going on ahead of me landing. Before Xmas I had a drink.

Nothing mental but I drank. I did this again on New Year's Eve. I'm sorry. I don't want to be this person. I feel like I've taken away every single apology I've made to you over those years when I was drinking heavily. I've been in contact with a rehab centre at home. I don't know if it's possible but I really think I should go away for a few weeks to get my head straight. It's really costly and I know I don't deserve it but I was wondering if I could take the money from my savings to do this? They said they'd have a bed for me tomorrow. I just have to talk to their doctor ahead of an assessment. Don't worry, I'm not drinking today, nor do I plan on doing so. I just wanted to have this out in the open so I can't change my mind on the flight".

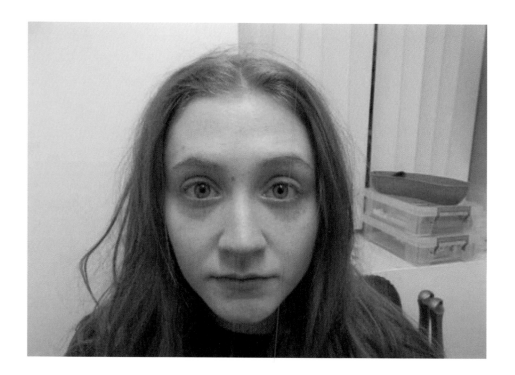

I stayed at my parents' house that night and by 4 p.m. the next day I was checked in for a month at my chosen rehab centre. I was in for a shopping list of issues: anorexia, self-harm, alcohol and my addiction to benzodiazepine. I said teary goodbyes to my mother and was escorted to my room.

My bags were searched and my possessions confiscated. No phones, no deodorant, no razors, no books, and much more. I was left alone to unpack. The tears just wouldn't subside. I wasn't upset about being there, I was just overwhelmed. Thankfully, I had the room to myself. After a while, my therapist came to my room and I was introduced to my 'buddy', Dee. After she showed me around my new home for the next 30 days, I met some of the other patients. As always, I was taken back by just how 'normal' everyone was. Two of the lads left the room pretty soon after I came in. I found out moments later that this was to google me, as one of them had a suspicion of who I was. It probably should've made me feel awkward but it only made me feel comforted by the fact I had less to explain about myself. As I was still emotionally disconnected, I was pretty content to just sit and get to know everyone.

Within days, I'd made really great friends with the other 11 patients and the staff. It wasn't until two weeks in that I hit a wall. My anxiety woke up before me. So, when I opened my eyes, I had a vision of me waking up every morning for the rest of my life. I watched it like a movie and suddenly I was exhausted at the concept of living. How could I possibly exist every day, as long as I lived? From that moment on, my feelings returned and I became aware of why they'd had to leave in the first place. I was controlled by self-hatred, a desire to die and a depression so deep that everything felt impossible. The only difference this time was I was finally in a safe enough environment for me to feel my true emotions. The closest I'd gotten to 'feeling' during my time there was when I was asked to sing karaoke on Saturdays. I made people cry with my rendition of 'Sober' by Demi Lovato, a song about relapsing. Singing has always given me the ability to connect with myself. That morning I confessed my thoughts of the morning in group therapy. The therapist asked if I was thinking about suicide to which I admitted, I was. There was no point in clearing out my life savings if I wasn't actually going to be honest, I thought.

After two days on suicide watch things began to change for me. I was learning how to cope with the voices in my head again. The turning point was an afternoon of drum therapy. Will, who had come to rehab the same day as me and quickly became one of my best friends and a true confidant, had got his hands on two African equivalents of a bass drum. This made playing loud easy. We were shouting the lyrics of a song in a foreign language and hitting the drums as loudly as we possibly could. The reason doctors encourage drum therapy is because it's impossible to play the drums if you are preoccupied with thinking – you have to feel the rhythm otherwise you lose it. In that lesson, I lost myself in the true childlike joy of living in the moment, having fun and playing music with a carefree abandon. No one had every suggested it before. My face hurt from smiling and my stomach ached from laughing so hard.

This continued long after the session had finished. Drumming had allowed me to connect with myself, and the essence of my issues. It made me naturally high. For the next few weeks, my fellow companions in rehab thought of me as the girl who skipped around the place. I would run around from class to class and hop around as I did so. My therapists told me never to lose that feeling. I felt like a teenager again – something I'd lost doing *The X Factor* at such a young age and having to grow up very fast. I was on the up and up, so I decided to check my emails one night. I opened up the link to my album work in progress and began to make notes of what I wanted to change. I was buzzing.

The feeling didn't last long. A nurse who was on call that night quickly turned the computer off. She instantly banned me from listening to music and checking my emails – not that I had access to it during the day anyways, as there was no television, radio or CD players. I apologised and agreed not to do it again. I was just so happy that I was excited about making music again, and that feeling was enough to keep me going. Naturally, this wasn't the only thing I got in trouble for in my time there. I'd been pulled up on my exercise, my isolation and my drinking of contraband coffee!

As much as rehab felt like a holiday camp from my life and responsibilities, it was also a place for me to become comfortable with the uncomfortable. I managed to fill an entire A4 notepad with anecdotes of my afflictions. With every addiction I confessed, I felt lighter. So also through talking to the other addicts. I felt less alone. After years of self-inflicted isolation, both emotionally and physically, I was again learning how to communicate in an open and honest manner. I learnt more about myself in a month of rehab than I'd ever managed in my 24 years on this planet. I got to see who I was without being tarnished by the outside world. I enjoyed my stint in there so much that when it came to go, I was sad. My aunt, bless her, even offered me money for an extra two weeks if I felt like I needed them. I said no. It was time to get back to my album. During my last week, I toyed with the notion of extending my stay. Upon a weekend of self-reflection, I realised that this was just my attempt at running from my problems that existed on the outside. No matter how long I stayed, they'd still be there, waiting for me. While I was overjoyed about my newfound lease of life, it was time to get back to work. I wanted so much to finish my album and this book. Everything that had at one point overwhelmed me to a point of stagnancy now seemed achievable and, most importantly, exciting. Music had always been what brought me back in my life. So, when I lost my passion for it by the end of 2018, I was petrified. It was my only constant. To imagine my existence without it was to also imagine a life without me in it. Music is all I've ever known and it's all that I need to make my life make sense.

Leaving rehab was scary, I had to adjust to the sensory overload of the colours that existed outside plain white walls. It took time, but it was all worth it. With my hand on heart, I can say I wouldn't change any of my experiences or choices up until that moment. They led me to the place that I am in now and for that I am grateful.

I cherish the friendships I have made and will mourn the people I've already lost to this illness. Every day is a blessing and I try my utmost not to take it for granted. I have my life back. After 10 years, I can finally close the book on these confessions. And I can't wait for what happens next…

AFTERWORD

Dear Reader,

If you're here reading this, then thank you for taking the time out of your own life to read the book of mine.

Today is a rainy day in late January 2020. I thought I'd update you as it's been six months since I finished writing the book, and today is the day I finished mastering the album too.

Everything has worked out. More than worked out, actually. Life's pretty blooming fantastic, if I'm being honest! Never in a million years would I have expected to be in the position that I'm in right now. I'm happy, healthy and holding my own out here in the big wide world. I couldn't be further from the me that you'll find in several of the stories in this book.

I'm now one-year sober for the second time (God willing the last time too). I visit my therapist regularly and, let's be honest, no one could get paid enough for that task.

I'm the heaviest I've ever been but also the happiest and the strongest. I'm enjoying having adventures with Bean, my Italian greyhound, and am also the owner of a Smart Roadster (which I've nicknamed 'Beep'). I hope to pass my driving test soon.

As for *Confessional*, my album, I couldn't be happier. Three singles so far! You could also say that I'm the proud mother of those confessions and songs too.

Every day is a blessing; I'm not taking anything for granted. I hate to sound like a tired cliché but I truly feel like I am living the dream. With every new song I release into the wild, I'm reminded of why I do this and how I'm one of the lucky humans who gets to do what they love every day.

If you will let me share one more thing with you, then it's this: if you are a sensitive soul, like myself, who feels like the world was not meant for you – that every day you are a burden to those around you and you believe they'd be better off if you weren't there – then let me tell you something for nothing: that's not true. I never believed that I would make it a day past 19 years old – but here I am.

I wanted to eradicate myself from the lives of others because I felt that happiness would never be attainable to me. How wrong I was. I'm now 25 and I wish I could go back in time and hug the younger version of myself. To tell her that it all works out in the end. That she is worthy, she is worthwhile and that she does deserve to take up space. She is not defined by the number on the scales, the scars on her wrists or the voices in her head.

Unfortunately, time travel does not exist just yet. So, I'm hoping that you might listen and learn from the mistakes that I made, instead of having to live them too. Life is hard and life is beautiful, but it is meaningless without the meaning *you* give it.

I turn my sadness into songs and my pain into prose. And I'm alive because of it.

Much love,

Janet

x

CAPTIONS

p.3:   Age 7, Holy Communion, Plumbridge. "It may have been my big day, but Gavin's Daffy Duck tie is stealing the show!"

p.5:   Age 18 months, family home, Gortin. "Were you even a child of the Nineties if your mother didn't dress you as a sailor?"

p.13:   Age 6, St Patrick's Primary School, Gortin. "Fun fact: I forgot my tie for this school siblings picture day!"

p.15:   Age 7, family home, Gortin. "When someone tells you to 'Smile!'"

p.31:   Age 18, Lough Erne, Enniskillen. "Let it slide, baby."

p.52:   Age 19, Insomnia HQ, Stevenage. "I hate the term 'Dead behind the eyes' but I'm dead behind the eyes."

p.67:   Age 21, Ware, Hertfordshire. [Photo by Alex Johnson]

p.74:   Age 21, Insomnia HQ, Stevenage. "Let me address the elephant in the room: I look like a giraffe. A very malnourished giraffe."

p.86:   Age 16, Megan Sweeney's house, Omagh. "Ashamedly so, I was actually smoking a cigarette in this photo, but it's been very well cropped so that you wouldn't know."

p.93:   Age 23, Warehouse, Stoke Newington. [Photo by Emma-Jane Lewis]

p.101: Age 19, Belfast City Hall. "Why learn to play an instrument when you can just sit in front of lots of amps and give the illusion that you're a musician?!" [Photo by Stephen Barnes/Alamy Live News]

p.105: Age 18, Insomnia HQ, Stevenage. "Sign your life on the dotted line…"

p.113: Age 1, Gortin. "Have you ever seen a child look more like a potato in your life?"

p.116: Age 15, Megan Sweeney's house, Omagh. "Yes, I went as the poor man's Lady Gaga for Halloween."

p.125: Age 20, Red Lion, New York City. "Red Lion, meet red lion."

p.129: Age 20, Top of the Rock, New York City. "Long-haired-person problems."

p.143: Age 20, with Graeme Pleeth at Abbey Road Studios, London. "Graeme is the true star of this photo! Also he said something wildly inappropriate right before this was taken, hence why I'm smiling so hard."

p.150: Age 20, New York City. "Nothing says 'tourist' quite like taking a picture in the middle of the sidewalk in NYC."

p.155: During the *X Factor* Live Tour 2012. "Did I put those holes in those tights myself? Yes." [Photo by Brian Rasic/Getty Images]

p.161: Age 19, Abbey Road Studios, London. "Topping up a long night of drinking with a celebratory drink."

p.167: Age 17, the *Twilight Saga: Breaking Dawn* red carpet. "Fun fact, I went to Nando's in this dress after!" [Photo by Jon Furniss/WireImage]

p.170: Age 24, RAK Studios, London. "A rare photo of me and JQ actually being serious and not silly!" [Photo by Daniel Ido]

p.177: Age 24, Smarmore Castle, Ardee. "I'll just have one drink, I'll be fine…"

p.183: Age 24, RAK Studios, London. "Smiling through the fact I don't have a clue what I'm doing!"

ACKNOWLEDGEMENTS

No one really warns you about how hard it is to write an autobiography, especially a book as intimate as this.

Sitting down and simply writing down the words would never have been possible if I didn't have the love from my family to fall back on, and to know that if it all ever became too much, I was always welcomed back home with open arms and huge hugs. I would like to specifically thank my mother, Patricia, for her "No dream is too big" attitude. She has truly kept me aiming for the stars. Thank you, I love you.

I want to give my resounding thanks and gratitude to all at my management team, Insomnia. Over the years I've given them too many sleepless nights to mention. To Cat and Rick, thank you for taking me into your home so that I could pursue this crazy dream of mine and for never giving up on me, even when I gave you many reasons to do so. To MJ, Matt and everyone else at Team Insomnia, thank you for believing in me when everyone told you I was a risk.

For Claire, I want you to know that not only am I overwhelmed with gratitude for your existence and your assistance, but also that you are truly an angel whose divine intervention saved me more times than I deserved.

To my best friend, Megan, thank you for giving me the belief in myself and always reassuring me that I can do this weird, wacky, wonderful "job".

I'm forever indebted to Malcolm Croft. Thank you for taking the time out of your already busy life to navigate my words. Without you, this book would never have come to fruition – you were the one who told me I can, and should, write this story. At this point I think you know me better than anyone as you've read over 100,000 words of my unedited prose.

I want to give a massive thank you to Graeme Pleeth. You've done more favours for me than I deserve and you're one of my favourite people to exist. *Ever.*

To the team at Omnibus, thank you so much for welcoming me into your lovely world and for believing in this book enough to publish it. Never in a million years would I have believed that I would one day become a published author, especially after talking all of your ears off for an hour during our first meeting! Thank you for signing this crazy person, I'll be forever grateful.

To my fans – allow me to call you my friends. This book would not have been possible without you. Your support and love is truly what keeps this leaky ship afloat. There were long and tough days when I was writing this when I just wanted to give up – but you were always there for me, cheering me on from the sidelines. Thank you for never giving up one me and for making my dreams a reality. This is all for you.

To all of the lovely people I've met in recovery, I want to say thank you. You've made my sober journey such a blessing and so much less isolated. Thank you to all of the folks I met at Smarmore – you know who you are. You all made such an impact, I will never forget you. Thank you. To Will, in particular, thank you for being my partner-in-crime when we were locked up in rehab. May we never have to play a game of Guess Who ever again.

Finally, I want to thank caffeine. This book would have most definitely not been possible without it.

Thank you, one and all…

DISCOGRAPHY

ALBUMS

Running with Scissors (2014)
Confessional (2020)

EPs

Duvet Daze (2015)
December Daze (2015)
Little Lights (2016)

SINGLES

'Suantraí Meisciúil' (2015)
'Outernet Song' (2016)
'I Lied to You' (2018)

FILM

Songbird (2018), lead role

CREDITS

'Confessional'
Words and Music by Janet Devlin and Nathan Thomas © Copyright 2019
Insomnia Music Management and Universal Music Publishing Ltd.
All Rights Reserved. International Copyright Secured.
Used by Permission of Insomnia Music Management and Hal Leonard Europe
Ltd.

'So Cold'
Words and Music by Janet Devlin and Paul Statham
© Copyright 2019 Insomnia Music Management and Warner Chappell Music.
All Rights Reserved. International Copyright Secured.
Used by Permission of Insomnia Music Management and Warner Chappell
Music.

'Saint of the Sinners'
Words and Music by Janet Devlin, Bradley Mair, Theo Weedon, Matt Weedon
and Jonathan Quarmby
© Copyright 2019 Insomnia Music Management, Matt Weedon, Theo Weedon
and Rak Publishing Ltd.
All Rights Reserved. International Copyright Secured.
Used by Permission of Insomnia Music Management, Seven7 Management
and Rak Publishing Ltd.

ABOUT THE AUTHOR

To millions, Janet Devlin will always be that flame-haired girl with the phenomenal folk voice who wowed the world on *The X Factor* in 2011. However, the real Janet is so much more. She is a multi-hyphenate of both creation (singer, poet, lyricist, author, actress, ukuleleist, vlogger) and destruction, as this book reveals for the first time.

In the years since her tenure on the hit TV show, Janet Devlin has been busy putting all her incredible creative talents to hard work, culminating in the May 2020 release of her hugely anticipated concept album, *Confessional*, a collection of 12 pop-folk anthems. The album is a statement of intent: "This is who I am – as an artist, and a human," declares Janet. It's a staggering union of songwriting and soul-searching.

Janet's previous album *Running with Scissors* (with song collaborations from big-hitters such as Newton Faulkner and Jack Savoretti, released in 2014) and subsequent follow-up EPs established Janet Devlin as something more real than just a former reality show artefact. She also generated thousands of supporters on Pledge-Music, her then-independent distribution channel. A plethora of opportunities arose during these years: she was invited to perform to 82,000 people during a Gaelic football match at Croke Park stadium, headline three UK and Ireland tours, as well as perform for His Holiness the Dalai Lama, whom she was also invited to meet personally. Not bad for a shy emo kid from Gortin, County Tyrone!

Building her music career on the foundations of independent artistic control, writing, recording and performing songs is just the tip of the iceberg of Janet's recent creative achievements. In 2018, she starred in a leading role in *Songbird*, a modern fantasy based on a fairy tale penned by award-winning screenwriter Tommy Draper, who created the character of 'Jennifer' especially for Janet. The film, and Janet's two original compositions for its soundtrack, picked up a string of awards, including Best Original Song at the Midlands Movies Awards 2019 and Best Foreign Theme Song (Artemis Women In Action Film Festival 2019), as well as receiving a nomination for Best Soundtrack at the Nexus Film Awards 2019.

Alongside this big screen success, Janet has also transformed into one of the UK's most influential YouTube creators on the smaller screen, garnering more than half a million subscribers since she first started posting content back in 2006. Her regular video creation includes the uploading of original music, cover songs, vlogs and poetry, as well as forthright and frank posts on topical issues including mental health, sexuality and bullying.

My Confessional is Janet's first book. She currently lives in London, is the proud mother to Bean (her Italian greyhound) and, despite indications to the contrary, maintains she is still the world's laziest perfectionist.